WE'VE MADE IT *ea*

CW00429970

beat

the

banks

Paul Lewis

The publisher would like to say a particular thank you to Jane Vass and Fran Gonsalves for their help in reviewing this book.

Published in 2008 by Age Concern Books

1268 London Road, London, SW16 4ER, United Kingdom

ISBN: 978 0 86242 431 2

A catalogue record for this book is available from the British Library.

Edited by Lyn Taylor

Cover design by Vincent McEvoy

Designed and typeset by Design and Media Solutions, Maidstone

Printed and bound in Great Britain by Bell & Bain Ltd, Glasgow

Author

Paul Lewis is a freelance financial journalist who
writes and broadcasts widely on personal finance
issues. He presents *Money Box* on Radio 4 and
his work also appears in the *Scotsman, Daily
Telegraph* and *Reader's Digest*. His other books
include *Money Magic* and *Live Long and Prosper*.

Contents

To my mother

Introduction

I like banks. I do, honest. They are really useful. And in some ways they do exactly what you want them to. First of all – and we are so lucky we can take this for granted – they provide a secure place to keep our money. (Please don't mention Northern Rock! If anything, the crisis there in September 2007 showed just how safe they are.) And second of all (as people weirdly say nowadays), they are there when we want to borrow more, pay bills or save up.

I recently joked on television that one particular charge made by the banks had clearly been dreamt up by the taking-money-off-people-without-them-noticing department. Within hours I had an email from a listener saying such departments did exist! His dad had worked for one. It was called the Retail Innovations Unit!

And although banks – and indeed the whole financial services industry – are heavily regulated (though confusingly not all the products they sell us are), they often seem to see the rules as a challenge to overcome rather than a framework to work within. They specialise in hidden charges, cunning arithmetic and complex rules that have lawyers scratching their wigs.

So this book is about getting your own back. Understanding the rules the banks and insurance companies (and fund managers, and brokers, and financial advisers and so on) play by. And spotting the scams (did I say scams? I meant, erm, subtle ploys) to part you from your cash. Preferably without you noticing – until it's too late.

This book is mainly about saving and a little bit about investing – and don't let anyone tell you they are the same. It is about making your money work as hard for you now as you worked to get it in the first place. Between us we lose billions of pounds a year by not keeping an eye on our money. Every penny should be sweated – from the £300 in your current account to the savings for your retirement.

I show how six people of modest means can be hundreds of pounds a year better off by making simple changes to their banking, saving and investing – and generally, without taking any risk at all.

This book also takes a quick look at financial advice and how that will change. And how to complain and get compensation if things do go wrong.

So it's all jolly interesting. But…

WARNING

If you have debt you should pay that off before you even think about investing or saving.

The reason is simple. You will never earn more by investing £1,000 than you are being charged to borrow it. Here's the arithmetic.

Scenario 1: You have a debt on your credit card of £1,000, and you have £1,000 in a savings account. On that loan, the bank will charge you, let's say, 15% a year. So by the end of the year you will have shelled out £150 in interest. And still owe £1,000. On your savings, a good bank may give you 5%. So at the end of the year it gives you £50 (and there may be tax to pay but more of that later, I'm keeping it simple as this is still the introduction). So at the end of the year, you have spent £150 – £50 = £100.

Scenario 2: You use the £1,000 in your savings account to pay off your £1,000 debt. So obviously at the end of the year, you have paid out no interest and earned none either. It has cost you nothing. So paying off your debt leaves you £100 a year better off than putting £1,000 to work when you also have £1,000 in debt. *So*

pay off debt!

That means pay off your credit card, get rid of the overdraft, and see if you can end any bank loans early without being charged penalties. Even paying off the mortgage may be more important than putting a bit of money into an ISA. Of course, most financial advisers will not tell you this; no-one earns commission when you pay off debt. But it is a vital thing to consider yourself before you save or invest a penny.

> A bank is a place that will lend you money
> if you can prove that you don't need it.
> *(Bob Hope)*

First thoughts

You get into debt when you spend more than your income but once you have paid that debt off (or you never had any), your income is probably a bit more than your spending. In other words you have excess income – or, to put it another way, money you haven't spent. This book is about that money.

It does not matter if it is a lump sum in a building society account, a slowly growing balance in your current account or used tenners stashed under your mattress. If it is unspent income, it is savings. This book will help you make that money work harder for you. Left to itself, money is a lazy creature – you have to put it to work and then you have to keep your eye on it to make sure there is no slacking. Interest rates change, best-buys come and go, investment deals change. If you do not check on what your money is earning, you will lose money. And the banks will make it. Trust me, they make enough already.

Now of course, sorting out your money is not as interesting as going shopping, walking in the countryside, or meeting a friend down the pub. But then, nor is working. One person who worked for me put it this way 'Paul, what you have to understand is that I only come here each day to fund the rest of my life.'

Looking after your money is just the same. A bit boring. But it makes sure you have more to spend – perhaps on your next romantic weekend away. And it just might fund some of the rest of your life.

Before we get on to the details, an important truth:

Investment and saving are very different. When you save money it remains yours. When you invest money, you give it to someone else to use. Generally, any investment puts your money at some risk. And, despite what financial advisers may say to you, risk does not always mean reward; all too often it means loss.

Cash savings

Cash is the first thing any of us saves – we put money to one side for a holiday, Christmas, or a new pair of shoes. Nowadays, people often do not do that – they borrow the money to buy what they want and then pay it back later. But all of us have saved up for something at some time, and however sophisticated our investment plans are, some of our savings will always be in cash, usually in a bank or building society account.

There are great advantages to cash:

- It remains your money and it is safe. Banks and building societies almost never collapse in the UK; and even if one did, they all belong to a compensation scheme which now protects all of your money up to £35,000 (see pages 101–102 for details of compensation).

- It earns interest – or at least it should. So your money will grow or provide an income.

- It is accessible. You can take it back to spend at any time. Sometimes you will lose some of the interest it has earned if you take your money out without warning, but that can be avoided.

This means that if you put £10,000 into your savings account, you know that you can get at least £10,000 out, whenever you want it, in the future.

These advantages also lead to the big disadvantage of cash. Nothing exciting happens. Your money does not grow very fast. And if you want your money to make you an income, you will take the interest out as it is credited and at the end of the year, or the decade, you will only have left what you put in.

Investments

Investment is saving's riskier cousin. It means giving your money to someone else to use in the hope that they can make it grow fast enough for both them and you to see the advantage.

They pay you for the privilege and say that they expect to return it to you at some time in the future. But you have to be careful. How much will they pay? Will they give it all back to you at the end? And even if they say they will give it back, can you enforce that promise?

When you invest, you buy assets – such as shares – and these assets are only worth what someone else will pay for them in the future. It is just like buying an antique chair or an old car. Just because the assets you buy are measured in pounds does not make them any different – or any safer. Your money is no longer yours. It is the asset you own and if you need to convert it into money you will only get what someone will pay at that time – less any charges.

There are good reasons to invest. Over the last 100 years, money that has been invested in shares has grown faster than money kept in cash or even money invested in 'fixed interest' investments, such as bonds. If the past is a guide to the future, then investment will be better than saving as a route to wealth. But there are problems:

- **Your money is at risk.** Some investments are safer than others, but ultimately they all depend on a company doing what you hope, an asset growing in value as expected, or the institution that looks after it doing what it promises.

- **Your money is inaccessible.** To get your money back, you will have to sell the investment to realise the cash. That will mean delays and, of course, costs. The selling price of something on a particular day is always less than the buying price – it's called profit or sometimes the 'spread' – so if you invest it today you will get less back tomorrow, even if the value of the investment has not changed. The value of investments goes up and down, so there are good and bad times to buy and sell. You have to be able to wait for – and spot – the good times.

- **Part of your money will disappear every year.** There will always be costs in any investment, partly to pay the salaries of the people who invest it and manage it. Some will make an upfront charge, taking maybe 5% of your money just for the privilege of taking you on as a customer. Then there will be an annual management charge. Nowadays, that is standardising at around 1.5%, although you will find instances of 1% or even less. But some kinds of investment will charge you a lot more.

- **We don't live for ever.** If we could invest over a century or more, then putting money in the stock market would be a very good idea. But over shorter periods, investing can mean that your money is worth less than when you put it in. In the summer of 2007, share prices fell and money you invested nine years earlier on the stock market would have been worth no more after those nine years. In the last 100 years, there have been two periods of around 25 years when shares were worth no more at the end than at the start.

Investment is also trickier than saving. Nowadays, the buzz phrase is 'asset allocation', which is just a fancy way of saying don't put all your eggs in one basket – especially when it's your nest egg. So it's not all about shares any more – it's about commodities, bonds, property, fixed interest, gilts and so on. Confused? The judgements you have to make in deciding where to invest your money, and how, are much more complicated than putting money into a bank account.

This book does not look in any detail at pensions. They are, of course, an investment. And the examples in the 'Beating the banks' chapter on pages 61–87 do include some examples of putting spare money into a pension. But they are such a huge subject there is not room to discuss them in detail in this book.

The inflation drain

When you see a financial adviser – see pages 88–102 for help with that – they will say that if you put your money in cash, inflation will eat away at it. For example, suppose you put that £10,000 in a savings account and spend the interest it earns. In 20 years time what will it be worth? Because it's cash, the whole sum will still be there to take out. But that £10,000 will be worth a lot less than when you put it in because as prices rise, what your money can buy falls.

Over the last 20 years, prices have risen by around 3.6% a year on average, which means that since 1987 they have just about doubled. If you had £10,000 in 1987, you would need £20,000 now to buy as much as £10,000 would have bought then. With inflation as it is now, the value of money halves about every 20 years. Even after 5 years £1,000 is only worth £832, and only £700 after ten years. So if you put your money in a savings account, when you take it out it will be worth less because it will buy less.

But the same is true of investment. Inflation affects money invested just as much as it affects money saved as cash. So inflation is not a reason to invest rather than save. Investment is only better if the money grows faster than it would in a savings account. And that does not always happen.

One problem with inflation is that there are now two official ways to measure it. The older measure

– called the Retail Prices Index (RPI) – is the one I use throughout this book when I refer to inflation. But the Government now prefers to use the new Consumer Price Index (CPI), not least because it is always lower. It omits certain items that are included in the RPI, such as housing costs, and the arithmetic is done differently. At the time of writing the RPI is double the CPI. It is the CPI which the Bank of England keeps to the target of 2%.

The tax cart

When you save or invest, it is always sensible to think about tax. Will the money your money earns be taxed? If so, at what rate? And will that tax be taken off in advance or paid later? But reducing or avoiding tax should never be the main reason for taking on a particular investment. Think of investing as a horse; it drives your finances forward. The tax you pay is the cart – the burden the horse pulls. A light cart will never make a lame horse go fast. So never put the tax cart before the investment horse.

The Government encourages us to save for the future by offering tax advantages on the money we put into pensions and other sorts of savings and investments. Every £78 we put into a pension is boosted by another £22 from the Chancellor (though this changes to £20 for every £80 from April 2008). Cash ISAs (Individual Savings Accounts) accumulate interest free of tax. And many National Savings products produce tax-free returns. But before investing in any of them, make sure that the investment itself is what you need and is sound.

Spouses (including of course civil partners) can save tax by planning their investments together. If one pays no tax, or is taxed at a lower rate than the other, assets can be transferred to that partner. Always make sure, however, that you think about the implications of death, relationship breakdown or bankruptcy.

You should always check that you are not paying too much tax on your savings or investments. If you do nothing, tax at 20% will automatically be deducted from the interest earned on your savings. If you do not pay tax on your other income, you can claim this tax back, or stop it happening. Remember that interest rates and returns are usually quoted before tax is deducted. If you have to pay tax, the actual return may be much less.

If you are thinking of retiring abroad, then tax becomes more complicated. You will normally be taxed only once on your money (normally in the country where you live, no matter where the income arises). But there are complications and you must take care.

Beware of offers to save money 'offshore'. The Revenue knows when UK citizens invest outside the country and will make sure you pay tax on any money the investment earns. Putting savings offshore can help you delay paying the tax in some cases. But for those of modest means, it is seldom worthwhile.

Finally, you should never embark on an investment just because there are tax advantages or be persuaded by financial companies to take on a scheme because of the tax savings. Make sure that it is a good investment without the tax breaks. The Government can always take them away in the future.

That's the end of the warm-up act. On with the show!

Saving

Current accounts

Before you even think about saving money, where is your current account? You know, the day-to-day money that comes in from your job, your pension, or that friendly relative in South Africa? (This book is full of dreams!) Because even that money should be working for you. The High Street banks have not come to an agreement about what interest to pay us on our current accounts (that would be illegal) but they do all pay much the same on their standard current accounts. The Big Five (HSBC, RBS NatWest, Barclays, Halifax Bank of Scotland, Lloyds TSB) normally pay a standard 0.1% a year. Now, if you have £1,000 in a current account and it pays 0.1% interest, then at the end of the year you get £1 – before tax. So that ends up as 80p for letting the bank look after your £1,000. Now your £1,000 is not sitting as a hundred tenners in a drawer. No. It is being lent by the bank to other banks and earning – at the time of writing – 6% or £60 a year. So the bank will keep £59 earned on your money and let you have the other £1!

 Money-making tip: *If your bank or building society does not pay interest on your current account, move it to one that does: 4% is easy; 6% is possible.*

But beware. The banks are after your money. And they are happy to trick you into putting it with them. Here are some common current account tricks.

- **Good interest on the first slice.** You get a higher rate of interest but only up to a certain amount. For example, you might get 6% but only on the first £2,500. Anything above that earns the standard 0.1%.

- **Minimum payment in.** Some banks will demand that you have a minimum amount going into the account – usually £500 or £1,000 a month – before it pays a better rate. Not everyone can do that.

- **Monthly fee.** Sometimes you will be charged a monthly fee. It will include things you don't want or need – such as insurance products – and is always a bad idea.

- **Better interest if you take another 'linked product' from the bank.** This is a marketing ploy for the other product rather than generosity to you. Say 'No'.

Generally, building societies are better than banks. They seem not to have noticed that all the banks have (separately) decided to pay 0.1% interest or less. They pay a variety of rates, some quite decent, and many have much higher upper limits for paying it – up to £250,000 or even £1 million in some cases.

Some banks that are exclusively on the Internet pay a reasonable (but no longer great) rate on almost any amount.

You can find details of the rates banks pay on one of the web-based comparison sites. See pages 36–38 for more on comparison sites and best-buy tables.

Moving your bank account should be straightforward. Your old bank has to tell your new bank about all the standing orders and direct debits that leave your account, and it should do that within five days. It must also cooperate fully in your move to the new bank. It can take three or four weeks to get it all sorted out, but can be well worth it. If you have regular payments into your account – for example from an employer, the Department for Work and Pensions, or a pension scheme – you will normally have to tell them the new details yourself.

Of course, the banks will tell you that a current account is not just about interest. It's about branches, cash machines, how quickly money is credited to your account and service. But this is all nonsense!

Branches

The banks have been busy closing branches for years and have rejected the sensible idea of sharing them – one premise, but each bank having its own counter. I'm not sure it matters terribly. Nowadays, the only people who really need a branch are those who pay in cash or, to a lesser extent, cheques.

Money-saving tip: *The banks that let you use the Post Office to pay in and take out money over the counter from your current account are: Alliance & Leicester, Bank of Ireland, Barclays (England and Wales*

only), cahoot, Clydesdale Bank, Co-operative Bank, Nationwide building society (cannot pay money in), Lloyds TSB (not in Northern Ireland), smile. In addition just about all banks will let you operate a basic bank account through the Post Office. Could they have made it more complicated? Possibly. But it would be difficult!

Some banks now allow you to use your local Post Office to pay in money, take out cash, and pay bills, all free of charge, although there may be an extra delay before money is credited to your account. If you live away from a town with bank branches it is worth changing to a bank that has an agreement with the Post Office and using that.

Money-saving tip: *If your local Post Office has a cash machine, it will probably charge you £1.50 or more to take money out of it. If you queue up and take it out over the counter, it will be free, as long as your bank is one that has an agreement with the Post Office.*

Cash machines

All banks now belong to the Link network and you can withdraw money free from any Link cash machine on bank or building society premises. However, a growing number of Link machines in garages, neighbourhood shops, motorway service areas make a charge (normally around £1.75). They are owned by private companies that make money by charging us to access our own cash.

The charge should be shown on the outside of the machine and on the screen before you put your card in. You can find your nearest cash machine – and what it charges – at www.link.co.uk.

 Money-saving tip: *Find out where the free cash machines are near you and always use them. Machines that make a charge are an expensive way to get hold of your own money.*

Money go-slow

When money is paid into an account – or taken out – it goes through what the banks call the 'clearing system'. Banks in the clearing system should take three working days between the money leaving one account and arriving in the other. Some banks add a day or so before giving you access to the money – and the clearing system also likes weekends and holidays off like the rest of us, so the standard three days can creep up to five or six.

The banks have promised to introduce a virtually instant clearing system for telephone and Internet banking in May 2008. It is not clear yet whether there will be a charge for it.

 Money-saving tip: *When you are paying money in or paying a bill always take account of the time that money – even cash – takes to clear.*

Service

The banks are right that service standards vary. But finding out which is best is very difficult.

Banks move call centres overseas and then back again, some are open longer hours than others. And when you go into a branch, the main objective seems to be to sell you something you did not go in to buy.

Seeing red

Even if you have no debt and are saving, you can still slip into overdraft – especially if you use your current account for day-to-day expenses but try to move excess money over to a savings account. Overdraft charges are very high. Some charge interest of around 20% even on an overdraft you have agreed. If you go overdrawn without having an arrangement, expect to pay up to 30%. Banks also make hefty charges when you go overdrawn without permission. There can be a charge for each day you are overdrawn – usually with a monthly maximum. And you will be charged every time a cheque, direct debit or standing order is due to be paid, whether the payment is allowed or rejected. These charges can be £35 a time and you can easily run up a huge bill.

These penalty charges may be illegal and are the subject of a test case in the courts. But that will probably not be finally resolved until 2010.

Money-saving tip: *If you think a charge is unfair or excessive, complain and ask for it back. If you are generally a good customer who does not break the rules you may get it refunded. Otherwise the bank will put your case in its pending tray until the courts decide the issue. But registering your complaint is important.*

If you think you may go overdrawn on your account always make an arrangement first. Even authorised overdraft rates vary enormously and some current accounts charge you a monthly fee just for using one. Avoid them. Some banks allow you to overdraw by a small amount – up to £250 in some cases – free of charge.

Money-saving tip: *If you think you will need to make use of an overdraft regularly, you should pick an account with a low interest rate on agreed overdrafts and keep below the agreed limit.*

Credit cards

When you open a new account the bank will try to sell you all sorts of stuff that you may or may not need or want. The safest thing is to turn it all down. You chose the bank for its current account; that doesn't mean its credit card or its loans are any good.

Credit cards in particular are best chosen to suit your own circumstances. Do you pay off your bill in full each and every month without fail? If so, then the rate of interest does not matter a jot. Instead you should find a good cash back card and use it for your shopping. Pay it off in full each month and get the cash back bonus. You can get 1% still with some cards.

Do you pay your bill in full most months but sometimes let it run on when you've bought something expensive? In that case, you should look at the interest rate and pick a card with a 0% rate for all new spending for the next few months.

Take it out and use that one for buying that new computer or sofa. Make sure you pay it off before the 0% offer ends. Best to put a note on the calendar at least a month in advance to make sure you don't miss the deadline.

Do you have a debt on your card that never quite seems to go away? Stop using the card. Take out a new card that offers 0% for balance transfers. Go for the longest deal. You will usually be charged a fee of at least 2% on the money transferred. Move your debt and work out how much you would need to pay off to clear it before the 0% offer ends. Never use the card for spending. In fact, cut it up with scissors the moment it arrives.

Alternatively, stop using the card and stop paying the minimum amount each month. Work out how much you can afford to pay and make a regular standing order to do that until the debt is cleared.

Another alternative is to take out a card that offers a low 'life of balance' rate on debt you transfer to it. You might get 5 or 6% and that is cheap borrowing. Transfer your debt, cut up the card and never use it and pay off the debt as quickly as you can.

Money-saving tip: *Whatever your credit card and however you use it, always, always make sure that your monthly payment is not late and never exceed your credit limit. Otherwise you will be fined £12.*

When you take out a new card you will be offered payment protection insurance to protect your payments should you fall ill or lose your job. Always reject it. First, it is usually a waste of money. It will seldom pay out to someone who is retired or over pension age. Second, if you really want it you can always get it cheaper from an independent insurance company. Use the Internet to see what you can get that is appropriate for your age and circumstances. See pages 36–38 for information on best-buy tables.

You may also be offered insurance to protect you against ID theft. Turn that down too. If your identity is stolen, the bank bears the loss not you. So why pay for insurance that will be of no financial benefit?

And you will probably be offered a service to register all your cards in case they are stolen. It is a complete waste of money. Firstly, because you can usually make the calls yourself on free 0800 numbers. Secondly, because as with ID theft, any actual losses are borne by the banks. They just want to charge you to reduce their loss.

Money-saving tip: *If you have insurances against ID theft, losing your cards or having them stolen, or protecting your payments if you are ill or out of work, get rid of them.*

When you stop using a credit card completely cancel it. If you do not, it may prevent you getting new cards in the future. And some card companies now charge a fee for cards that remain completely unused.

Direct debits

And just before we leave current accounts, a word about direct debits. I am a fan. They are one of the most useful services the banks offer us. Some people are scared of them. But there is no need. With direct debits, the bill is always paid on time. That avoids penalties. And most utilities, such as gas, electricity or telephone providers, charge lower prices to customers who pay by monthly direct debit. So you can save money just by agreeing to it. The banks' Direct Debit Guarantee means that if a payment is made wrongly, the bank will reimburse you. Of course you must make sure that you have enough money in your account to meet the payment on the day it is due. If you are in doubt about being able to do that, do not take out direct debits.

Money-saving tip: *Arrange to pay all your regular bills by direct debit.*

Savings accounts

There are more than 3,000 savings accounts to choose from but it is not hard to work out which is best for you.

The first and most important thing to look at is the rate of interest that will be paid on the money you want to save. After all, it is about money and how much you make and you can get more than twice as much with the best as with the average. To make the comparison, look at what is called the AER or Annual Equivalent Rate. That makes sure the comparison takes account of how frequently the interest is paid. The bigger the AER number, the better the account.

Second, you have to consider when you want the interest paid. If you want a regular income from your savings, then you will want your interest credited every month or perhaps every quarter. But if you just want the money to grow and do not need to spend the income, then choose an account with interest paid annually. Interest paid monthly is always slightly less in total than annual interest on the same account, because you have had the money earlier. But still use the AER to compare (the AER shows the rate your money would earn if the interest paid was not taken out but left in to the end of the year).

Third, will you operate your account exclusively over the Internet? Normally, the very best interest rates are confined to online accounts.

Fourth, how long do you want your money tied up for? In the past, the longer you tied up your money or the more you saved, the higher the rate of interest you could earn – not any more! You can get top rates on savings for amounts of £1 with instant access to your cash without penalties, especially if you operate the account over the Internet. You can sneak a few fractions of a per cent more by tying up your money for three months or even three years. But there is not much in it.

Money-making tip: *Some of the best savings deals are with the banks, not the building societies. But if you are a long-standing member of a society, do not close your account completely. Keep your*

account open with a small amount of money – say around £100 – in case the society converts to a bank or is taken over by another building society. That should ensure you get any windfall that is paid.

Beware of savings accounts that appear near the top of best-buy tables because they offer an 'introductory rate' – in other words, they pay you more for six months or a year but then drop down to a much lower rate. Normally, around half of the top ten rates in the best-buy tables are there only because they offer a bonus for six or twelve months. Some best-buy tables separate out the accounts with and without a bonus. All of them warn you if there is a bonus. Always stick to the accounts that have no bonus, unless you are absolutely sure that you will swap again when it runs out.

One of the new tricks the banks have come up with on savings accounts is to offer interest rates that seem very high – until you look at the small print. Recently, one offered 12% if you put money in regularly by direct debit each month. But the new rate only lasts for a year and so most of your money never actually earns 12%. Overall, these accounts earn about half the advertised rate. Beware of such tricks. Go for a simple, no-nonsense rate that is paid on the first pound and does not have special conditions or short-term bonuses with it.

The biggest trick of all played by the banks is changing their deals. They tempt customers in by offering good rates of interest and then letting them drift downwards over the years until they are rubbish. When I last looked, there were 2,369 instant access savings accounts. The top ones pay more than 6%. Once you get past the top 50, they are paying less than 5%. So the remaining 2,319 are rubbish! Some pay only 0.1%.

Money-saving tip: *Check the interest paid on your savings once – preferably twice – a year. Chances are, the best-buy this year will be an also ran in a year or two.*

Finally, remember that the interest you earn on current or savings accounts has 20% tax deducted from it automatically. If you are at least 65 and your total annual income is below £7,550 (and £9,030 in 2008/09) you should pay no tax; you can claim back the tax that has been taken off you and register to have your interest paid gross without tax being deducted in future. These figures apply to people aged 65 or over. They are slightly higher if you are 75 or over and considerably lower if you are under 65. Even if your income is higher – up to £11,000 or so in 2008/09 – it is possible that you should be paying tax at 10% on your savings income. You can claim back the difference. If you have a joint account and one of you is a non-taxpayer then half the interest can be paid without tax deducted. If your bank or building society refuses to do this, complain.

Money-saving tip: *If you are in a couple and one of you does not pay tax, move money into the non-taxpayer's name – as long as you trust each other. Remember, the money will become theirs and if you split up they do not have to give it back to you.*

For more details on age allowances and tax on savings and the latest rates and allowances, see the Age Concern book, *Pay Less Tax*.

Internet banking

If you have a computer and an Internet connection, you can get the best deals for your money by moving your bank or building society accounts to an Internet-only account. Some people are afraid of using the Internet in this way. But you should not be. Internet accounts are safe and secure if you are careful. There are crooks around the world who send out emails pretending to be from your bank and asking for your security details. Always ignore them. Your bank should never ask for information in this way. Treat them as you would someone standing near a cash machine who asks for your PIN. Never click on an email attachment unless you know and trust the person who has sent it. Attachments can contain software that steals data as you enter it.

Internet accounts normally pay better rates of interest and charge lower rates on overdrafts than branch-based accounts. Internet accounts also put you much more in charge of your money. You can look at your account, move money around, check your balance, and see what payments have come in and gone out, 24 hours a day, 365 days a year (366 days in 2008!). (Now don't spoil things by mentioning Northern Rock again! Yes people had problems accessing their accounts online. But I say again, no one lost any money. Except the poor old shareholders. But as I explain later, shares are risky.) If you have any queries about your account or want to change the way you pay bills, you can do it all through the computer. And most have a telephone helpline as well in case you get stuck.

Of course, there are some disadvantages. Older computers may not have the necessary security to operate the account so you will need an up-to-date one, as some older computers cannot run the software required. You will also have to be connected to the Internet and pay the costs of that – broadband makes life a lot easier, at a relatively small monthly fee. You will be expected to look at bank statements online. But you should always print out a copy for yourself once a month and file it. Some Internet banks do not let you have a chequebook, so all payments have to be done electronically through the computer. Remember that even though the money will leave your account immediately, at the moment, it will still take three or four working days to reach another bank (see 'Money go-slow', page 14).

Money-saving tip: *If you haven't tried Internet banking, why not open an account and put a bit of money in it to see how easy it is? If you like it, then you can think of transferring all of your money.*

Offshore accounts

Most UK banks offer what they call 'offshore' savings accounts. These are usually at branches or subsidiaries located in the Channel Islands or the Isle of Man, and offer reasonable rates of interest with the advantage that the interest is credited gross, without tax being deducted. Some banks have marketed these accounts as 'interest paid without tax deducted', giving some customers the impression that they do not have to pay tax on the interest. Or at least, can avoid it if no one asks.

Not any more. Recently the Revenue won a court case giving it access to the records held by the UK banks of all their customers who have an account located abroad. The Revenue is working its way through the list and at some point you will be found.

 Money-saving tip: *Offshore is not really a good idea unless you are very rich, totally dishonest or both!*

If there is more than a small amount in an offshore account, some delay may occur after death before probate is granted (in other words, before the will is approved and the dead person's assets are released).

Cash ISAs

Individual Savings Accounts (ISAs) replaced TESSAs for cash savings made after 5 April 1999. TESSAs no longer exist – the last one ended in 2004.

There are two types of ISA:

- a cash ISA, which is a savings account where you can save cash, and

- an investment ISA, where the money will normally be at risk on the stock market.

This section deals with cash ISAs. Investment ISAs are dealt with on pages 53–55. If you want to put money into an investment ISA that may affect the amount of money you can save in a cash ISA.

In 2007/08 you can put up to £3,000 into a cash ISA (sometimes still called a mini-cash ISA), which is really just a savings account on which interest is paid. And in 2008/09 you can put in £3,600. An ISA account has two big advantages over other savings accounts:

- The interest is free of tax. You do not even have to tell HM Revenue & Customs about it.

- Interest rates tend to be slightly higher than for other investment accounts. So even if you are a non-taxpayer, a cash ISA paying a high rate of interest may be a good idea.

You can take your money out of an ISA at any time without a penalty and still keep the tax relief on the interest it has earned. The only restriction is that you cannot pay in more than the limit during the tax year. So if you put in the maximum £3,600 in April 2008, you can take out £1,000 in, say, November but you cannot put any more in until the next tax year begins in April 2009. However, if you put in only £2,000 in April 2008 and take out £1,000 in November, you can put another £1,000 back in – and another £600 if you want to – as you will then have put in the maximum £3,600 for 2008/09. You can have more than one cash ISA. But the limit is not for each ISA, it is the total paid into all ISAs during the year.

The best ISA accounts are the simple ones. It is always best to find the highest-rate ISA that pays the same rate of interest from the first pound, with no bonuses that run out after a year.

 Money-making tip: *If you have some money on deposit and you are a taxpayer, put it into an instant-access ISA. The interest will be tax-free and you can take the money out at any time.*

Fixed-rate accounts

All the accounts mentioned so far have a variable rate of interest – in other words, as interest rates set by the Bank of England rise and fall, the rate you are paid on your money will rise and fall too, although usually not at the same time and often not by the same amount. Fixed-rate accounts are different. They guarantee you at the outset that your money will pay a fixed return for a fixed period – for example, 6.15% a year over three years. Some pay the interest monthly or annually, others at the end of the period. You have to agree to leave your money in for that length of time. If you take it out early, you will be fined. Or as the banks would say, lose some of the interest already paid. Even cash ISAs can be fixed rate in this way.

These products are sometimes called 'term accounts' or 'fixed-rate bonds' – but beware, because the word 'bond' can apply to many sorts of investment. Some, like these, are completely safe. But the word is also used for other products that are very risky.

There are two advantages to fixed-rate accounts:

- When interest rates are low, you may well be offered more than the rate you can get on a variable rate instant access account. But when interest rates are expected to stay much the same or fall you cannot gain more than a quarter of a per cent or so even by investing over three years.

- You know exactly what your income will be, even if interest rates change. If they fall, then you will be getting a good rate.

And three drawbacks:

- You have to invest a minimum amount – usually £1,000 or more.

- Your money is tied up for a specified time. If you take it out before then, you will pay a financial penalty.

- If interest rates rise, your return may not seem so good. You are gambling about future interest rates. If they fall, you win the gamble; if they rise, you lose.

 Money-making tip: *If you are really sure you have money you will not need for a fixed period, consider a fixed-rate cash bond or account. Make sure the extra you*

get is worth the risk. If you need the money, you will pay a penalty.

See pages 36–38 for more on best-buy tables and comparing bank accounts.

National Savings & Investments

Despite its name, all 'National Savings & Investments' (NS&I) products are 'savings'. Some are long-term and one mimics a stock market investment. But with NS&I your money is never at risk because the Government backs it. That means all its products are as close as you can get to an absolute guarantee that your money is safe. You can get income, capital growth, protection from inflation, or take a gamble with Premium Bonds. Some NS&I products pay out tax-free and so are good for taxpayers, especially if you pay higher-rate tax. With others, the interest is paid gross but is taxable. That is good for non-taxpayers who do not have to pay tax on it – and even for taxpayers who get to keep the money until they sort out their tax at the end of the year.

But it is very important that you buy a product that suits your tax status. There is no point in investing in a product which pays out tax-free if you don't pay tax and don't expect to in the future.

I like NS&I products because of their variety and safety and sometimes they offer very good deals. You can now buy some of them in some branches of WH Smith. They are seldom recommended by financial advisers because NS&I does not pay commission.

Savings certificates

If you want tax-free capital growth over a fixed period of two or five years with complete safety, then National Savings certificates may suit you. For example, the 37th issue 2-year bond pays 3.95% tax-free. Because it is tax-free, that is the same as earning 4.93% interest that is taxable if you pay basic-rate tax. And if you pay higher-rate tax you would need to earn more than 6.58% taxable to beat it.

Some certificates are 'index-linked' and pay an interest rate that is a fixed amount above the rate of inflation. Currently, they pay 1.35% above inflation over two or five years. If inflation stays over 3%, then this is an excellent return, especially for higher-rate taxpayers.

You can invest anything between £100 and £15,000 in each savings certificate. If you cash the certificate in early you will be charged a stiff penalty. At the end of the period you will be asked what you want to do with your money. If you do not respond, it will be reinvested for you in a similar product and may well be tied up again for some time.

Pensioner guaranteed income bonds

If you are 60 or over, you can get a regular monthly income and a reasonable rate of interest from pensioner bonds. The interest is taxable and rates are not exceptional. You need at least £500 to invest (the maximum is £1 million). The rate of interest is guaranteed for one, two or five years. You run the risk that interest rates will rise and you will be stuck with a bad rate. There are tough penalties for cashing in early.

Income bonds

If you are under 60, you don't get such a good deal. Income bonds offer a variable rate rather than a fixed one. They pay a monthly income which is taxable but it is paid gross – so you will have to pay the tax through self-assessment or PAYE. Interest rates are generally no better than OK-ish. You can do better elsewhere.

Children's bonus bonds

These bonds for children under 16 are usually taken out as five-year savings plans by grandparents or other relatives. The interest received is free of all tax and offers a guaranteed annual return over five years. They come in £25 units and the maximum you can buy for each child is £3,000-worth for each issue.

Premium bonds

Premium bonds are a gamble. But it is only the interest you are gambling with (you can get your original capital back at any time). Instead of paying everyone the interest earned, it is all pooled into the prize fund each month. That is then divided up into two £1 million prizes, a few hundred prizes in the thousands, about 20,000 prizes of £500 and

£1,000 and about 1.5 million prizes of £50 and £100. If you win a prize it will almost certainly be £50.

The rate of interest is currently 4% and prizes are paid tax-free. But about a quarter of the fund goes on the very high prizes that you will probably never win. So the real rate of return is about 3% and even for a higher-rate taxpayer that is only worth about 5%.

Nevertheless, a great many wealthy individuals do have the maximum £30,000 in premium bonds. (The minimum purchase is £100.) They would normally expect to win 17 prizes a year, normally of £50. But even they have to wait more than 49,000 years to have an even chance of winning £1 million!

Guaranteed equity bonds

National Savings & Investments guaranteed equity bonds are a risk-free way of getting returns like those on the stock market. If the value of shares rises you get that growth. If it falls you will get your original investment back or a bit more. (The deals vary but some guarantee to give you more than 100% of your original investment, whatever happens to shares.) There are no fees or charges. Your money is normally tied up for five years. So the risk you run is that the stock market falls, or rises very little, over that time and your money would have done better on deposit. But you can never lose money. The bonds are not always available and each issue is slightly different. You can register to be told of the next issue on a form from the Post Office or through the NS&I website.

Cash

Normally NS&I is not a good place for cash. The savings account is rubbish and the minuscule amount of interest it earns is also taxable. But at the moment, its Direct ISA is excellent and well worth a look. Avoid the cash mini-ISA, which is not so good.

 Money-making tip: *Always check out NS&I products when you want to save up, especially over a fixed period.*

Government stock (gilts)

We're taking tentative steps towards the foothills of investing. But we are still in what I classify as savings territory because there is no risk. It is called government stock, generally known as 'gilt-edged securities' or 'gilts'. And that's not the first odd word we shall come across.

You lend your money to the Government and it guarantees to give you all your money back at a certain time. Until then, it pays you interest at a fixed rate twice a year. The interest is taxable but is normally paid gross and you will have to pay the tax on it.

The Government sells gilts in 'certificates' with what is called a 'nominal' value of £100. The certificate has a 'redemption date', which is the date on which you will be paid £100 for it, and a 'coupon', which is the rate of interest paid each year on that £100 value.

For example, 8% Treasury Stock 2013 promises to pay the holder of a £100 certificate £8 a year in two instalments of £4 on 27 March and 27 September and give the holder £100 on 27 September 2013.

These particular certificates were first issued in April 1993 when interest rates were 5.75% and expected to rise. Today, earning 8% on your money is very attractive and people who bought them then are doing well now. You can still buy this stock. But to get a £100 certificate you would have to pay more than £100. In August 2007, for example, its price was £117 – and if you bought it for that you would still get £8 a year, paid in two instalments, which is a return on your £117 of around 6.8%.

It still sounds attractive but you have to take account of what happens when the stock reaches its redemption date. In September 2013 you will only get back £100 for a certificate that cost you £117. So you will have lost £17, and that must be taken off your interest payments over the time you hold it. Taking that into account you get what is called a 'redemption yield' – which is a measure of the real overall return on your money. The arithmetic is complex, but in this example, it would be about 5.2%.

The *Financial Times* publishes lists of all government stock each day, together with their yields. You can also see them on the Debt Management Office website.

Most gilts pay interest twice a year, so you can build up a savings package of six different gilts, paying in different months, to secure an income each month.

If a gilt has more than one date – such as 5.5% Treasury Stock 2008–2012 – the Government decides when to redeem it between those two dates.

You can also get index-linked gilts. Here the interest rate is lower (typically 2.5%) but both the interest payments and the final value of the stock is index-linked – in other words, each year you get more than £2.50, and at its redemption date you get £100 plus inflation for each £100 certificate.

You do not have to hold the gilt until its redemption date. You can sell them at any time – in the same way you bought them. If interest rates have risen since you bought the gilt, the price of each certificate will be less than you paid for it. If rates have fallen, it will be more.

There is a group of stocks which have no redemption date. The Government can choose when – or if – it buys them back at face value. Generally that means no-one wants to buy them and if you hold one of these 'rump' stocks you are stuck with it.

You can buy and sell gilts through banks, some building societies, stockbrokers, and by post using a form available at Post Offices. Using the postal service, you pay 0.7% on the first £5,000, subject to a minimum of £12.50 for purchases (no minimum commission for sales), and £35 plus 0.375% on any amount over £5,000. So you would pay £12.50 commission if you invested £1,000, £35 commission for £5,000 invested, and £53.75 for £10,000. On sales, you would pay, for example, only £1.75 commission on proceeds of £250, £17.50 on £2,500, and £44.38 on £7,500.

The postal service is usually cheaper than other methods but there will be a delay between your signing the cheque and the money being invested so you may end up getting less (or more) for your money than you were expecting.

Money-making tip: *Consider putting some money into gilts if you want safe predictable returns.*

The Debt Management Office administers gilts and produces a free booklet called Investing in Gilts: The Private Investor's Guide to British Government Securities. *You can find out more and download the guide at www.dmo.gov.uk.*

Best-buy tables

With all this choice, your head is probably spinning. There are more products to choose from than the human brain can process. Luckily, there are several websites to help us find what are called 'best-buys'. These best-buy tables are useful but not perfect.

- Most tables charge the product providers – the banks and insurance companies – to appear on their lists. Small product providers cannot afford the fees the websites charge. For example, many accounts offered by small building societies or credit unions are not listed because they will not pay those fees.

- Some tables let product providers pay for adverts so their products appear at the top of the best-buy lists. Although these are clearly marked off – or should be – they can mislead users into thinking that a product is the best performer when it is not.

- Some product providers choose not to be included. That is particularly true in insurance comparison sites. For example, online insurer Directline chooses not to take part in best-buy tables. And you will not find gilts in there nor many National Savings products for the simple reason that the Government does not pay for them to be there.

- The comparison websites can exclude some products for their own reasons. For example, the Indian bank ICICI offered the best interest rate on a cash savings account for a long time but was excluded from some lists because it was not a member of the Banking Code (see pages 89–90 for details of the Code).

The websites also make money from us using them. Every time we click on a product to find out more, the product provider pays the website a fee. And if we buy something from that website, they pay them a bigger fee. Despite the problems, best-buy tables are indispensable when we are trying to find an account that pays the best rate of interest or an insurance product that is the cheapest. But you must be careful.

Banks and financial companies devise products that will get to the top of the tables rather than offer us a genuine best-buy. That is why savings accounts offer a bonus rate for a year. That can get them into the top ten. But when it ends, they slip back to 35th place, hoping we won't notice. As I write this, top of the cash ISAs in some lists is an account that appears to offer 8.1%. But to get it you have to open another investment with the same amount of money and the overall return will be much lower. We have to beware of those tricks.

 Money-saving tip: *Use several comparison sites to find the best deal. Do a search rather than just read off the best-buy list they present themselves. Be sceptical. And look at the deal in detail before committing a penny to it.*

 Three of the best-known comparison websites are www.moneyfacts.co.uk, www.moneysupermarket.com and www.fool.co.uk, which also has a lot of useful explanations and articles. If you do not have access to the Internet, MoneyFacts *is published each month as a magazine and your local library should have a copy. The FSA also publishes some best-buy tables free of commercial links.*

Later in the book, we will see how six ordinary people can be hundreds of pounds better off by following these simple ideas. But first I want to take you on a scary trip around investing.

Investing

So far we have looked at saving – where what you get is guaranteed. And how you can beat the banks by moving your money around and getting the best deal. But now we are coming into the dangerous territory of – roll of drums and small fanfare – Investment. Where nothing is what it seems and money can be lost. This section does not pretend to list every investment you can make. But it does give a rough guide – together with some warnings.

Shares

For most people, investment means buying shares in companies – in other words, investing in the stock market. From 1975 to 1999 the value of shares went up year after year. Even though the price fell in three of those years, the next year prices bounced back higher than before. So putting money in shares seemed a one-way bet to wealth. But from the start of 2000, shares fell. This century, people have learned the hard way the truth of the warning that the value of shares can go down as well as plummet. The overall price of shares on the London Stock Exchange fell by 10% in 2000 and then by another 16% in 2001, and again by 25% in 2002. The fall continued until 12 March 2003, when the price of shares was less than half its value at the peak when the millennium began. Then, finally, the market began to rise again. Share prices ended in 2003 nearly 14% higher and they rose again, by rather less, in 2004 then by more in 2005 and rose again in 2006. Heady stuff. As I write in 2007, shares have plunged and rallied and are round about where they began the year.

So four years after they hit bottom, share prices are about 90% up on their 2003 nadir. Hurrah! But they are still as low as they were more than eight years earlier. Boo! In other words, if you invested in shares in the middle of 1999 your money will not have grown by one penny as at mid-2007. Over the last 100 years, shares have fallen in four years out of ten. Nevertheless, most financial advisers will say that investing in shares – they normally use the posh word 'equities' – still has an important part to play in any long-term investment strategy.

A share is literally a share in the ownership of a company. Put simply, if the company is worth £1 billion and you own one share of £1, you own a billionth of the company. There are two ways to make money by owning a share.

1. Income

The company may pay you a dividend which is a share of the profit the company has made. If the company makes profits of £100 million and there are a billion shares in issue, then for each share, the company has made 10p. As a shareholder you might get about a fifth of that, say 2p. The rest would be reinvested in the company. The return on investments in the stock market currently averages around 3.5% a year – in other words, if you buy shares worth £1,000, the dividends you get will be around £35 in the course of a year. That money is taxable but is paid with basic-rate tax already deducted.

2. Capital gains

The value of the share may rise. That means you can sell your share for more than you paid for it and make a profit. As long as your total capital gains in the year are less than £9,200 (in 2007/08), you pay no tax on that. Of course, the value of your shares may fall, as they generally did in 2000–2002, so if you sold them you would get less than you paid for them. But that loss is only made when you sell the shares; if you hang on and share prices rise, then you may find that the losses are reversed.

Indices

It is the rise in the value of shares that has been the main source of wealth for stock market investors. You will often hear rises and falls in UK share prices reported on radio and TV or even in the newspapers, as a movement in 'the Footsie'. That usually means the FTSE 100 index, which is produced by the *Financial Times* and the London Stock Exchange (hence FT-SE). It measures the movement in the value of shares in the biggest 100 companies on the Exchange. This index rises and falls each moment the stock market is open, as the prices of shares change. The figures I use throughout this book on how the stock market in London performed are FTSE 100 figures.

Another index is the FTSE All Share index. Contrary to its name, it does not include all the shares listed on the London Stock Exchange, but only those in about 700 companies which are actively bought and sold (some companies have very few shares or they are all owned by a few people who do not sell them).

Each stock market has its own indices, such as the Dow Jones Industrial Average ('the Dow') for the New York Stock Exchange, the Nasdaq Composite for the 5,000 or so companies that trade on the Nasdaq, and the Nikkei Stock Average of 225 shares on the Tokyo Stock Exchange.

I mention all this partly because I love every toggle on my anorak and partly because it will come in handy (promise) when we discuss investments called 'trackers' that follow these indexes.

Investing in shares

Before reading this section, do remember there are lots and lots (and lots) of ways of investing that do not involve shares. Some of these are mentioned later. And many of the things I say about funds of shares also apply to these other things.

Because the value of shares in individual companies is so unpredictable, most people put their money into a fund that has shares in a wide range of companies. The theory is that as some fall, others will do well, leaving the fund value rising. Investments in these funds are usually sold through what is called a 'unit trust'. The investor buys a number of 'units' in this fund and will get a return that depends on the overall growth of the money in the fund. Some funds pay out these gains as income, while others just let it accumulate and you have to sell units to realise money from your investment.

Most funds are run by a team of highly paid people who study the market and move the money around, trying to find the best returns. These are called 'managed' funds. Sometimes the word 'actively' is added to make it sound like people are rushing around and doing a good job looking after your money – if only!

Others are called 'tracker' funds. These simply buy shares in all the companies that are in a particular stock market index, such as the FTSE 100, the Nikkei Stock Average or the Nasdaq. They are called 'tracker' funds because their value should follow or 'track' the index. But investment professionals like to call them 'passive' funds. That makes them sound as if the money is just sitting there passively doing very little. Not true either.

So once you have decided to invest some money in shares, the next big decision is whether you want your fund actively managed by a team of experts or do you want to hitch your money to the overall performance of the stock market with a tracker?

To me it's a 'no brainer', to put it into the modern vernacular!

One big advantage of tracker funds is that, because tracking takes far less work than managing, costs are a lot lower and that is reflected in lower charges for you. And they have another huge advantage – they normally make a better return than managed funds.

It surprises people but, on average, the money in managed funds grows more slowly than shares in the whole stock market or the companies in the FTSE 100. Of course, every year some managed funds will do better than the market as a whole – they 'outperform' it, in the jargon. But you never know at the start of the year which funds those will be. The Financial Services Authority has produced research which shows that past performance is not a good predictor of future performance – with one exception. Funds that performed badly tended to continue to be bad. But funds that did better than the market did not tend to show 'persistency' of that performance over a number of years. So choosing a fund on the basis of how it has done in the past is certainly no guarantee of success in the future.

The main thing that determines how well a fund does is the overall performance of the stock market and the prevailing economic conditions. It also depends on the costs and charges that are eating away at your money and on the skill – and luck – of the fund manager.

Even if you do pick a fund that performs well, it is largely a matter of chance. There is no magic formula to choose among the 2,000 or more which are available. You can invest in a particular part of the world (UK, Europe, USA, Asia, Japan); in a particular kind of company (technology, start-ups, retail) and in vaguer things such as 'special opportunities', which basically means cheap shares that the fund manager thinks might just come right in the next year. You will also find 'cautious managed' – which may mean that the share selection is a bit like a tracker but with higher charges. You can try 'global growth', which means shares all over the world that the fund manager hopes will grow (why else would you invest?), or perhaps take a chance on 'emerging markets', where results can be spectacular but regulation is weak. Remember too that terms such as 'extra income', 'money builder' and 'high yield' reflect hopes, not promises, and you cannot complain if they do not happen. Or you can, but it won't do you any good.

You will seldom see past performance figures in adverts – partly because it is variable but mainly because of strict rules to stop funds being selective. One claim you do still see is that a fund has performed in the 'top quartile'. That means the fund is in the top 25% of funds of its particular type. They forget to tell you that over the long term, 80% of funds fail to beat the overall growth in the stock market. In other words, trackers are generally in the top 20% and so are well within the top 25% which are counted as 'top quartile'.

Despite the concerns of the FSA and the evidence about past performance, many people still want to make their judgement based on how well funds have done over the last few years. They may be misguided but it is factual information, not opinion, and if you want to adopt this approach, the information is published in the monthly magazine *Money Management*, available from newsagents.

The FSA also produces tables which include useful information about charges and terms and where funds can be bought. They are available at www.fsa.gov.uk/tables.

Ethical funds

If you are concerned that your money may be used for things you disapprove of, you could put it into an ethical fund. You can choose to avoid such things as tobacco, alcohol, animal experiments, weapons or pornography. Or you can positively choose to support companies with good environmental policies. These funds can produce as good a return as funds which are blind to such considerations.

Trackers

Trackers came to prominence when the value of shares rose year after year. Putting your money in the 'index' – in the FTSE 100 for example – avoided the risk of picking the wrong managed fund and seemed a safe bet. But after falling indices in three of the last ten years, their popularity has waned. Advisers will tell you that trackers follow the index down as well as up, which is true. What they don't tell you is that managed funds generally follow the market down too. And the evidence is that trackers do as well as or better than most managed funds with your money, even when the market is falling.

In a perfect world, the value of a tracker should precisely follow the index it uses. So if the FTSE 100 grows by 5%, your money in a FTSE 100 tracker should also grow by 5%. Three things stop trackers following the index precisely:

- Some buy a representative selection of shares rather than all of them. That avoids the cost of buying a few shares in small companies when a new investor joins the fund.

- When the companies in the index change they do not immediately get rid of the old shares and buy the new ones, which can be expensive.

- Buying and selling shares costs money. And there will also be the annual management charge. These charges are partly offset by reinvesting the dividend income that accrues from the shares to the fund.

So funds that track the same index can perform differently. A fund that does better than the index is as worrying as one that does worse; it means it is following the index approximately and has had some luck. A fund that does the job well will probably carry on doing so.

Exchange Traded Funds

One good way to hitch your money to the value of all shares is through an investment called an Exchange Traded Fund (ETF). An ETF behaves like a tracker fund but is in fact a company that buys and sells shares. It buys them so the shares the company owns reflect a certain index, such as the FTSE 100. Shares in an ETF are bought and sold like any other share. But there are two cost advantages over other shares:

- The buying price is the same as the selling price – in other words there is no profit on the deal – called the 'spread'. That can be as much as 7% on units in a unit trust.

- The Government does not charge Stamp Duty when you buy them. On other shares it charges half a per cent.

You can buy ETFs that follow various share indices, including the FTSE 100 of course, or indices which measure other markets in the UK and abroad. You can even buy an ETF which follows non-share investments, some of which are listed below. ETFs are cheap and efficient, but they are generally not recommended by financial advisers because – you've guessed it – ETFs do not pay commission. Charges are low – annual management fees are around half a per cent. You can buy ETFs like any other share. See 'Picking shares yourself' on page 52.

If you have ethical concerns about your money, you can track 'ethical indices', such as FTSE4GOOD.

Money-making tip: *If you want to invest some money in shares then an Exchange Traded Fund which follows the FTSE All Share or 100 index is a good way to begin. Remember you must leave your money there for a good few years.*

Not shares

There are lots of other things you can invest in that are not shares. In fact good investment advice stresses the need for 'asset allocation'. In other words some money in shares, some in cash and some in other stuff. Normally you have to buy the other stuff through funds. They can be managed or some of them will be trackers if there is a suitable index. With some managed funds, part of the money you invest will be in these non-share investments.

- **Commodities** – real things that are bought and sold, such as gold, coffee, timber, oil.

- **Currency** – some funds buy and sell currency in the hope of making a profit.

- **Debt** – some organisations make their money out of taking on debt and selling it on. That was one cause of the 'sub-prime' mortgage crisis that began to emerge in the middle of 2007.

- **Hedge funds** – they buy and sell the future value of various other investments.

- **Property** – commercial property is now easier to invest in through Real Estate Investment Trusts or REITs. Many major property companies have converted themselves into REITs, which means your money rides on the success of the commercial property market in the UK.

- **Fixed interest** – some funds buy gilts or bonds backed by Governments.

- **Companies** – although shares are the most common way to invest in companies, you can also do it through what are called 'corporate bonds'. These pay a fixed amount at a fixed time but the risk is the company will go bust and not make the payments. These are often recommended as a low-risk way into investing in companies, but they are not and should be avoided.

Charges

Whatever fund you choose, the pot you save your money in will have a little hole in the bottom through which a small but steady drip makes you poorer. It is like trying to run on a slippery road with a piece of elastic tied to your belt. You need a lot of energy just to stand still. Three powerful forces pull your money back:

- **Initial fees** – many investments will make an initial charge or entry fee. That takes some of your money away before it is even invested. It can be from 0% to 7%.

- **Spread** – this is the difference between the selling price and the buying price (sometimes called the 'bid' and 'offer' prices). The turn or mark-up is of course at the heart of business. It means that if you buy an investment at £100 but you only sell it back at £95, you have lost 5% immediately. The spread in a unit trust is normally between 5% and 7%.

- **Annual charge** – most funds charge an annual fee to 'manage' your investment and it will be levied whether the managing is good or bad. These charges were forced down by the Government but they are now on the way up and 1.5% is typical. Some are higher. So it is worth looking around to find charges of less than 1%. Trackers – and especially ETFs – have low charges. Aim for 0.5%.

When assessing charges, look at what is called the Total Expenses Ratio or TER. Even this does not include absolutely all the charges, but it is a better guide than the annual management charge, which omits some costs.

Money-saving tip: *In the uncertain world of investment, charges are one thing you can control. The level of charges should be a major factor when you decide where to invest your money.*

Parting with your cash

You can put a lump sum of £500 or more, or a regular amount of £25 a month or more, into a unit trust. Prices of units in the funds are published daily in newspapers and weekly or monthly in the financial magazines. Two prices are given: the lower or 'bid' price is the one at which you sell back the units to the company; the higher or 'offer' price is the one at which you buy them. You can get big discounts by buying them yourself from a financial supermarket (also known as discount brokers). These can most easily be found through the Internet – there is a list of them on the website www.find.co.uk. They are registered as Independent Financial Advisers to sell you financial products, but they do not give advice. You agree that you will deal with them on an 'execution only' basis. As a result, charges are low and any upfront commission they earn for selling you the product is paid back (they call it 'rebated') to you. They are a very cheap way of investing if you are confident about what you want to buy.

Picking shares yourself

Some people decide to pick shares themselves and buy and sell them directly, doing away with funds, managers and their charges. It is risky and you have to keep an eye on your investment all the time. You can buy and sell shares directly using online discount brokers. They offer no advice. If you want to make your own investments:

- spread your risk but avoid investing in too many individual companies, because of the monitoring and paperwork required

- watch your investments carefully and frequently

- never invest more than you can afford to lose.

 Money-saving tip: *To find out more about investing before risking a lot of money, why not join a share club? You can meet up with similar people and invest a small amount each month. Find out more from www.proshareclubs.co.uk.*

Tax

Tax considerations should not drive your investment or savings decisions, but by making full use of your tax allowances you can save a lot of money.

A couple may be able to save tax by transferring investments to the partner who does not pay tax, or who pays it at a lower rate.

If you are increasing your income through your investments, be aware of the impact this can have on your age-related Personal Allowance.

Most financial advisers will not be aware that people over 65 can pay an effective rate of tax of 30% or 33% on income between £20,900 and £25,835 – slightly more if you are aged 75 or more, and more still if you get Married Couple's Allowance. (These amounts will change in 2008/09 – see the Age Concern book *Pay Less Tax* for up-to-date rates.)

Individual Savings Accounts (ISAs)

ISAs began in April 1999 and are a simple way to invest money tax-free. They replaced PEPs (Personal Equity Plans) for new investments from that date. Anyone with a PEP taken out before 6 April 1999 can still keep it but from April 2008 they will be renamed ISAs (see page 55).

An ISA is not an investment in itself. It is simply a way of holding an investment so that the interest and growth are free of all UK tax (except for basic-rate tax on share dividends). There are maximum amounts you can invest in an ISA and they change from April 2008.

The Government calls Individual Savings Accounts (ISAs) that are invested on the stock market 'stocks and shares ISAs', even though they are investments, not, as the name implies, savings. And the phrase 'stocks and shares' is misleading because your money does not have to be invested in stocks and shares. It can be invested in bonds, in gilts, in REITs, in hedge funds or even in some sorts of cash funds.

The maximum limits for ISAs change from April 2008.

- **2007/08:** the maximum that can be put in an investment ISA is £7,000. All of that can be in an ISA that is invested in shares and other investments – called a 'maxi-ISA'. If you want to spread your risk you can put some money into a cash ISA (see pages 25–27) up to a maximum of £3,000. The other £4,000 can then be put in an investment ISA. Both of these are called 'mini-ISAs'.

- **2008/09:** the maximum that can be put into an investment ISA is £7,200. All of that can be in an investment ISA or you can put up to £3,600 of that amount into a cash ISA and the balance can be put into an investment ISA. The names maxi- and mini-ISAs will be scrapped.

There is no fixed term to an investment ISA. You can invest and can take your money out whenever you wish. The only restriction is that you can put in no more than the maximum during the course of the year. However, like any other investment, an ISA should be left for the long-term, see pages 59–60.

ISAs are billed as 'tax-free', but since April 2004, tax at 10% is automatically deducted from the dividends paid on shares and this cannot be reclaimed. So the tax advantage on shares ISAs is only for higher-rate taxpayers – who escape higher-rate tax on the dividends – and for those very few people who might otherwise have to pay Capital Gains Tax on the growth in their investment.

For most ordinary investors, the tax-free status of ISAs invested in shares is of no advantage. However, if you are considering an investment ISA, it is worth remembering that the tax advantages do still apply to ISAs invested in corporate bonds, REITs, gilts or other fixed interest investments. The income earned is free of tax and saves you paying basic-rate tax and any higher-rate tax. So if an adviser recommends a 'stocks and shares' ISA, remind them that it can also be invested in other investments that do have a genuine tax advantage.

Most unit trusts and other investments in funds can be bought using an ISA up to the annual limits.

Personal Equity Plans

Tax-free shares investments before 6 April 1999 were called Personal Equity Plans or PEPs. Anyone holding a PEP at 5 April 1999 was allowed to continue to hold it, but not to add to it. On 6 April 2008 PEPs will become investment ISAs. That will not affect your 2008/09 ISA allowance.

Annuities

One way of providing yourself with a definite income for the rest of your life is by purchasing an annuity. You give a lump sum to an insurance company and it gives you a guaranteed income for life. When you die, the income dies with you, and if there is anything left of the lump sum, the insurance company keeps it.

These 'purchased life annuities' should not be confused with the annuity you have to buy with a pension fund. Although they are the same in principle, they are treated differently for tax purposes. With a pension fund annuity, the whole of the income is treated as taxable. That is done because all contributions into a pension are free of tax, so the Treasury takes its tax when the income is generated.

A purchased life annuity is counted in a different way. Part of the money you get each month is treated simply as a return of your capital and is not taxed. Only the extra money – in effect the interest your money is earning – is counted as income and is taxed. HM Revenue & Customs decides how much is taxed, depending on your age and sex; the older you are, the more of your money is tax-free.

If you buy an annuity, you must make several decisions:

- **Flat or rising** – a flat annuity will be fixed for life; after 20 years of inflation, it would be worth far less than at the start. A rising annuity will either keep up with inflation (which at the moment is still measured by the RPI, not the CPI, see pages 6–7) or will rise at 3% or 5% each year. Of course, it will start off far lower, and taking the total income received over your lifetime, it is usually much better to take a flat annuity. However, a flat annuity will be worth less each year and if you live much longer than the average you will end up poorer and on a low income in your very old age.

- **Guaranteed or not** – do you want the annuity to pay out for a guaranteed period even if you die meanwhile? Buying a guarantee of five years will cost you almost nothing and will be good for your heirs.

- **One life or two** – if you are married or live with a partner, you can ensure that the annuity – or a fraction of it – continues to be paid to them if you die first. This choice will of course reduce the income from your annuity.

- **Impaired life** – if you are a smoker or have a disease that is expected to shorten your life, then you will get a higher income from an annuity.

- **Market-related** – although annuities are normally paid as a definite sum each month, some of them are now related to a fund that is invested. As a result, these annuities can go up and down as the fund does better or worse. They should be avoided.

The minimum sum required to buy an annuity is around £5,000; much more with some companies. The income may be paid in arrears or in advance, half yearly, monthly or annually. How much you get from each £1,000 of capital depends on:

- your age

- the insurance company chosen

- the conditions of the annuity

- interest rates at the time of purchase.

The amount you get as income from each £1,000 – called the annuity rate – has fallen by almost half over the last 15 years. That is partly because interest rates have fallen, and partly because people are living longer. The difference between the best and worst annuity is considerable, so choose carefully. Once you have bought it, you are stuck with that decision for life.

An annuity that pays an income for a short fixed term can be useful to bridge a gap before an improvement in your circumstances. If, for example, you are made redundant at 60 but your pension is paid from the age of 65, your redundancy payment could provide an annuity income in the meantime.

More complicated investments

There is one golden rule of investment – if something seems too good to be true, it probably is. There are many tempting offers in financial services that promise guarantees of high returns at little risk. People are always tempted, and advisers are always there to tempt them, but they are best avoided.

- **Investment bonds** are in fact life insurance policies which you pay for by one premium at the start. They are often sold on the basis that the income and growth is 'tax-free'. However, tax is in fact paid by the insurance company, so any return you get is after that tax has been paid. Their main attraction is that they generate high commission for the adviser – 7% is not uncommon.

- **Guaranteed income bonds** provide a guaranteed income but you need at least £5,000 and the money will be tied up for one to five years. The more money and the longer time you invest for, the better the return. Returns are paid monthly or yearly with basic-rate tax deducted. Only good for taxpayers.

- **Friendly societies** offer 10-year savings schemes with tax relief. They come with life insurance whether you need it or not. The charges are anything but friendly and returns are not great.

- **With profits policies** are a weird invention of the life insurance industry. They produce capital growth rather than income but what you get at the end is completely unpredictable and you may be charged a fine for leaving early.

- **Venture capital trusts** could be the next financial scandal. They were sold mainly on the back of tax breaks, which is always a bad idea. Those breaks have now been cut and VCTs are hard to sell on.

- **Investment trusts** are companies which buy shares and you buy a share of that company. They are freer to take risks than unit trusts and can also borrow money which can boost their performance. Not for beginners.

- **Open-ended Investment Companies** (OEICs) seemed a good idea but have failed to take off. Common outside the UK, they are a simpler and cheaper way of investing than unit trusts or investment trusts.

 Money-saving tip: *Avoid these products. They are not all bad but none are very good and they are not necessary.*

The long view

Where you invest – and whether you invest or save – depends on how long you want your investment to last rather than how much you have to invest. Before you invest – especially in the stock market – remember that it is a long-term decision. There is no point in investing money for a year or two. That is not investment – it is gambling. Anything less than 10 years is too short to count as an investment. Over shorter periods, money invested in shares runs a real risk of making a loss. Not least because you have to recover the charges levied at the start and the effect of the spread. Some people say that the long term really should mean 25 years or more.

So if you do invest money, make sure it is money you do not want or need for 10 years or more. And remember that, however long you invest for, it is always possible you will not get back what you have put in.

Money-saving tip: *Do not be tempted by investment unless it really is for you. With interest rates and returns where they are, cash can often be the best option.*

Beating the banks

Investing and saving seems tricky. But it's not. Here's how six typical people rearranged their finances to 'beat the banks'. These people – and their money – are all fictional and were devised using interest and tax rates that were current in summer 2007 using information from MoneyFacts and other sources. Every effort has been made to be accurate but deals change. Always check current rates and conditions before moving your money.

The packages are for sums from £13,800 to £36,000. Some of the investors are married and some are single; some are working and some retired. The youngest is 55-years-old and the oldest is 70. They all have fairly modest amounts of money, yet the improvements can be dramatic by making sure that every penny is worked as hard as possible, maximising the interest earned and minimising the tax paid. They involve little or no risk and almost all the extra income is guaranteed.

These six savings packages must not be taken as firm recommendations even if your circumstances appear to match the examples. Always consider fully your own needs before saving or investing, and take professional advice where appropriate.

Summary

Name	Age	Status	Non-investment income	Total amount to use	Savings aims
Ron	55	Single, employed	£19,000	£13,800	Higher income, some capital growth, reducing tax
Millie and Desmond	65	Retired	£16,935	£14,500	Increased income, no risk, reducing tax
May	55	Single, employed	£24,000	£16,200	Capital growth, higher pension, reducing tax
Nooreen	70	Widow	£5,000	£24,000	Income and safety money, reducing tax
Ed and Meg	60	Ed works, Meg doesn't	£32,000	£26,000	Capital growth, reducing tax
Mary and Sean	65	Just retired	£28,000	£36,000	Income, reducing tax

1. Ron

Ron is 55-years-old and earns £19,000 a year. He belongs to his company pension scheme. He has to make mortgage payments of £400 a month, but these end when he is 60. He has had savings of £9,750 in an Abbey Investor 60 account for many years. Despite rises in interest rates, Abbey pays him just 2% on his savings. His salary is paid into his Barclays current account. It pays only a nominal 0.1% interest on the current balance which averages £800 over the year. In 2004, Ron had a TESSA, which matured. He asked Barclays what to do and he agreed to its suggestion of a Barclays TESSA-only ISA (TOISA). He transferred the capital, spending the interest the TESSA had earned on a new sofa. It currently earns 4.96%. He has no other investments or assets apart from his house. He is happy to rely on his pension when he retires at 60, but wants to earn a bit more interest and pay less tax. He does not need the income from his savings. He would rather save it up until he retires.

Ron's original savings package

	Invested	Interest rate	Amount received	After tax	Notes
Current account	£800	0.10%	£0.80	£0.64	Barclays current account
TESSA only ISA	£3,250	4.96%	£161.20	£161.20	Barclays
Savings account	£9,750	2.00%	£195.00	£156.00	Abbey Investor 60
Total	£13,800		£357.00	£317.84	Apart from his TOISA, Ron pays tax on all his interest

Ron beats the banks

Ron's first step is to move all his money out of the Abbey account. He has to wait 60 days, or pay penalties. He writes to Abbey and waits for the cheque. His ex-TESSA is worth £3,250 and has always been long-term savings for when he retires. So he looks around and finds that Halifax is offering a fixed-rate ISA that lasts for four years at 6.27%. He calls into a Halifax branch to open one and says he wants to transfer the money from his Barclays TOISA. That paperwork will also take a little while.

While he is in the branch, the Halifax adviser asks about his current account. Ron has heard that High Street banks are not good for interest on current accounts. But when he says his net income is more than £1,000 a month he is told that Halifax will now pay 6% on the balance up to £2,500. Ron is never overdrawn, but if he does need to borrow a bit he will only be charged 15.9% as long as he authorises it first. So Ron moves his current account there too.

When his money arrives from Abbey, he decides to put the maximum £3,000 into a mini-cash ISA to earn interest tax-free. He chooses the National Savings & Investments Direct ISA, which pays 6.3% with instant access and no penalties. He can operate it over the phone.

For the rest of his savings, he decides to try out an Internet account. He looks at ING Direct which advertises 'one great rate'. But finds to his surprise that it only pays 5%. A quick search finds lots of better places and he plumps for the Coventry 50 plus esave account, which pays 6.4% and that rate is guaranteed for a year even though there are no restrictions on taking the money in or out. He can review it next year. He puts £4,000 in his new account to see how it works out, but he wants to keep the remaining £2,750 in a branch-based account where he can use a passbook or a cash card. He looks around again and once more, Halifax turns out best, paying 5.75% on its branch saver account, which he can access easily.

	Invested	Interest rate	Amount received	After tax	Notes
Current account	£800	6.00%	£48.00	£38.40	Halifax high interest current account
TOISA moved to fixed rate ISA	£3,250	6.27%	£203.78	£203.78	Halifax fixed rate 4 year maturity bond
Variable rate ISA	£3,000	6.30%	£189.00	£189.00	National Savings & Investments
Online account	£4,000	6.40%	£256.00	£204.80	Coventry 50 plus esave
Branch savings account	£2,750	5.75%	£158.13	£126.50	Halifax branch saver account
Total	£13,800		£854.91	£762.48	**Ron gains £444.64 a year or £8.55 a week**

Commentary

Ron has more than doubled the income his savings bring in, gaining £444 a year, partly because a lot of it is now tax-free. He anticipates letting that build up for his retirement, which he hopes will be in his early 60s. Next April, he can move another £3,600 into a mini-cash ISA to earn more tax-free income. He can also move his existing £3,000 as well if he finds a better rate somewhere else. His accounts are mainly with Halifax – which surprised him but the numbers spoke for themselves. He is pleased with the absolute safety of National Savings & Investments and glad he has joined a growing number of his friends doing some banking online. If he likes using the Internet account, he may want to shift more money there – if the interest rate stays high – and spend less time popping into his branch.

2. Millie and Desmond

Millie and Desmond are both retired. Millie stopped her part-time job last year when Desmond reached 65. Embarking on retirement, they want to maximise their income. Desmond has a company pension of £9,120 a year, which will rise with inflation. They both have a State Pension – Desmond's is £95.60 a week, which includes a bit of SERPS, and Millie has £54.70 based on Desmond's contributions plus a small amount of graduated retirement benefit from her work in the 1960s. Their mortgage is paid off.

They have £12,000 from Desmond's pension lump sum together with a bit of savings. It is in a building society account in Desmond's name with Alliance & Leicester; but despite the 30-day notice to get the money out, it only earns 4.05% gross. They also have a current account with HSBC, which is normally around £2,500 in credit. They like to know they can write a cheque for any sudden expense or treat. They are not greatly concerned about capital growth but want their

£12,000 to boost their pensions, which come to a shade under £17,000. They do not want to take a risk with this money. They want access to some of it but think they can afford to tie up around half of it, maybe a bit more, for a few years.

Millie and Desmond's original savings package

	Invested	Interest rate	Amount received	After tax	Notes
Current account	£2,500	0.10%	£2.50	£2.00	HSBC current account
Savings account	£12,000	4.05%	£486.00	£388.80	Alliance & Leicester phone saver
Total	£14,500		£488.50	£390.80	Tax paid on it all

Millie and Desmond beat the banks

Millie and Desmond look at ways to increase their income. The first thing to do is to move their current account. They never go overdrawn, have a reasonable balance averaging £2,500 over the year and all their pensions are paid direct into the account. They do not have a computer so an Internet account is out of the question. They decide to move their current account to Alliance & Leicester. Its Premier Direct account pays good interest on amounts up to £2,500 as long as you have £500 a month going into it, which they do. They decide to keep a bit less in their current account – £1,500 seems about right.

They consider the bank's DirectSaver account too which appears to pay 6.3%. But there is a hefty penalty if you withdraw money from it. So they reject that. Next door to Alliance & Leicester is Nationwide. They call in and find its monthly Income 60+ account pays 5.86% with no catches. As it is a joint account and Millie pays no tax, they register on form R85 to have half the interest paid without tax being deducted, and that saves a few pounds as well.

	Invested	Interest rate	Amount received	After tax	Notes
Current account (joint)	£1,500	6.13%	£91.95	£82.76	Alliance & Leicester Premier plus current account
Joint savings account	£4,000	5.86%	£234.40	£210.96	Nationwide 60+ monthly income account
Cash ISA	£3,000	6.21%	£186.30	£186.30	Kent Reliance BS, by post
Fixed rate savings (two years; Millie)	£6,000	6.55%	£393.00	£393.00	Saga two-year fixed savings account
Total	£14,500		£905.65	£873.02	**Millie and Desmond gain £482.22 a year or £9.27 a week**

The next step is to find a cash ISA for £3,000 of savings. They want instant access and they have heard on the radio that Kent Reliance is very good (Chatham girl Millie likes that!). They enquire and decide on a postal ISA account paying 6.21%.

That leaves £6,000 to invest for a bit longer. They think about National Savings & Investments but realise they can get a lot more from a Saga bond fixed for two years and paying interest monthly, which works out at 6.55%. It is taxable, so they decide to put it in Millie's name so no tax is due on it – they are aware that this means the money is Millie's and not 'theirs'. The bond ties the money up for two years and then they can reassess.

Commentary

Millie and Desmond have gained more than £480 a year (£9.27 a week). They think the banks have been well beaten by choosing products with higher interest rates and paying almost no tax by using tax-free savings and making use of Millie's tax-free allowance. Nationwide is the biggest building society and they prefer that to a bank. They are pleased with the deal from Saga. They must keep that money untouched for two years. The savings package also allows plenty of cash, including in their current account, for holidays, gifts, or other spending, but all their money is earning something.

3. May

May is a 55-year-old single woman who earns £24,000 a year. She keeps about £1,200 on average in her current account. She has savings of £10,000 in a building society postal account paying 2.35% gross, and £5,000 in a bank that pays 2.71% but offers a cash card and instant access. May wants to use her £15,000 to provide her with more money when she retires, which she does not expect to do until she is 65. She is prepared to lose some current investment income to provide capital growth.

May's original savings package

	Invested	Interest rate	Amount received	After tax	Notes
Current account	£1,200	0.10%	£1.20	£0.96	NatWest
Postal savings account	£10,000	2.35%	£235.00	£188.00	Leeds Capital 7
Instant saver account	£5,000	2.71%	£135.50	£108.40	Halifax Instant Saver
Total	**£16,200**		**£371.70**	**£297.36**	

May beats the banks

May is getting some income from her two accounts, but could do better. If she wants capital growth with safety, she will have to put at least part of her money elsewhere. The first step is to move her current account so that her day-to-day money earns something. Her standard NatWest account pays 0.1%. May is a computer buff and she is happy to do all her banking online in future. So she moves her current account to cahoot without a chequebook, which pays her 3.75% on the balance. Cahoot recently cut its rate from 4% and May could do better but she doesn't mind, she wants a purely online bank.

She puts another £3,000 into a cash ISA and again she wants instant access. She has read a lot about ING Direct and seen their adverts. So she goes with their Cash ISA which pays a reasonable 6%. That is tax-free, and next April she can move another £3,600 to the cash ISA. She decides to put that into a savings account and finds that cahoot will pay 5.75% on savings so she puts £3,600 in that ready for next April and tops it up to £8,000. May is already nearly £300 better off – another bank beater! – and she still has £4,000 she can invest for capital growth. She is happy to tie it up for 10 years until her anticipated retirement, but wants to be able to get it out after five years 'just in case'.

May should check her company pension scheme. It may be that her employer will match any extra contributions she pays in. If so, she should pay more into that. If not, she should pay into a personal pension. She can pay in as much as her salary each year, but she cannot afford that so she just uses the whole £4,000 left from her savings. She gets the money in before April 2008 so the Chancellor adds £1,128 tax relief, making £5,128 in her pension fund. That will be invested on the stock market and, as she is already over 50, she can take a pension from it at any age she chooses – and a quarter of it can be taken as a tax-free lump sum.

She plans to leave it in until she is 65. But if she wants to move it in five years to another pension plan she can do so. She chooses a stakeholder fund which has low charges, 0.75% a year, and tracks the FTSE 100 stock market index. All share investments are a gamble, but despite some market wobbles in the middle of 2007 May thinks over 10 years, this is a pretty safe approach.

	Invested	Interest rate	Amount received	After tax	Notes
Current account	£1,200	3.75%	£45.00	£36.00	Cahoot – no cheques
Cash ISA	£3,000	6.00%	£180.00	£180.00	ING Direct cash ISA
Savings account	£8,000	5.75%	£460.00	£368.00	Cahoot savings account
Total income				£584.00	**May is £286.64 a year better off – £5.51 a week**
Stakeholder	£4,000	5.00%*	£256.41	£1,384.62	Tax relief + 5% growth*
Total	£16,200				**And she has gained £1,128.21 tax relief into her pension fund**

*5% growth not certain.

Commentary

May is more than £5 a week better off – £286 over the year – through placing her cash and current account more sensibly and as much as she can tax free. She has also invested some money for her pension in the future and gained more than £1,100 tax relief. Next year, she has £3,600 to spare to put into her cash ISA.

May has a useful mixture of cash, which is safe, and of money in a pension fund, which is on the stock market. That money is at risk, but charges are low and if the market grows, her money will grow with it, and over 10 years she is confident that it is a good place for it. Of course, the market may fall. But as the Chancellor has added 28% to it, the chance of it falling below the total she invested herself is remote. May assumes that her fund will grow by 5% a year after charges. That is not interest and is not certain. But if it does – and it is a reasonable hope – then she will have gained £1,384 in year one from tax relief and growth. At that rate, the fund will be worth £6,500 after five years and £8,300 after 10 years for an outlay of £4,000. She will be able to take a quarter of that, more than £2,000, as tax-free cash and the rest she can use to buy a small pension for life. Of course, it may not grow that much. Five years is not really long enough to be sure it will even grow at all. But even if her fund does not grow at all over 10 years (unlikely but possible) she will have had the tax relief upfront and will not lose on the deal.

4. Nooreen

Nooreen is a widow of 70, with one daughter and two grandchildren. She has £24,000 that she and her late husband Navtej saved up. But she has to spend some of it to make ends meet and has never really taken much notice of it or the income it earns. She is just glad when she gets a bit added to her account once a year. It is all languishing in a Lloyds TSB Instant Gold Savings account earning 1.45%. Old accounts like this that are no longer marketed may have been good in the past, but are now terrible.

Her State Pension is £100.25 a week, which includes her late husband's SERPS. She used to draw it in cash each week from the Post Office, but then opened one of the new Post Office card accounts, and she still pops down there each week to draw it out. It is very little to live on and she finds it easier to use cash. She has tried to get more in the past. A few years ago she looked into claiming Minimum Income Guarantee, but as her savings were above £12,000 she was told she did not qualify. The rules for Pension Credit are different. Nooreen hears about this from one of her friends and calls the Pension Credit helpline on 0800 99 1234. She is delighted to discover she is

Nooreen's original savings package

	Invested	Interest rate	Amount received	After tax	Notes
Current account	£0	0.00%	£0.00	£0.00	Post Office card account
Savings account	£24,000	1.45%	£348.00	£278.40	Lloyds TSB Instant Gold Savings monthly interest
Total	£24,000		£348.00	£278.40	She pays tax on all her interest

now entitled to an extra £12.17 a week, despite having £24,000 savings.

Nooreen starts to think about her savings and how hard she and Navtej worked for them. She thinks that a higher income for the same amount of savings would give her the opportunity to use the extra money in different ways: perhaps a few extra gifts for her grandchildren.

Nooreen beats the banks

Nooreen's main objective is to increase her income. Her money could earn more almost anywhere. She is cautious and does not want to lose any of her capital. She does not use a computer and likes to be able to go into a branch of her bank or building society. She decides to open a Barclays current account and have her pension paid into that instead of the Post Office card account, which she closes. She can still draw money out of the Barclays account at a Post Office over the counter without paying a fee. Nooreen doesn't tend to leave much money in this account; she draws the money out each week as it arrives. She also opens a Day-to-Day Savings Account with Barclays and puts £4,000 of her £24,000 into that. It gives her 4.52% and pays the interest monthly, which she can draw out free with a cash card from any bank cash machine. She takes the radical decision to start spending some of this money – say £500 in the first year. After all, she won't live for ever and her daughter always tells her she does not expect to inherit any money. But she does like to give the grandchildren a treat now and then. The adviser at Barclays asks her about tax. Nooreen's income is low enough not to pay any so she registers to have the interest paid gross.

	Invested	Interest rate	Amount received	After tax	Notes
Current account	£0*	0.10%	£0.00	£0.00	Barclays current account
Savings account	£3,750**	4.52%	£169.50	£169.50	Barclays Day-to-Day Savings Account
One year bond	£10,000	6.37%	£637.00	£637.00	Birmingham Midshires fixed rate bond
Three year bond	£10,000	6.25%	£625.00	£625.00	Lloyds TSB term deposit bond monthly interest
Total	£23,750		£1,431.50	£1,431.50	**Nooreen boosts her monthly income by £96.09. She is £1,153.10 a year better off**

*Nooreen takes her pension out at once so she never has anything in her account. **On average. She runs it down from £4,000 to £3,500.

For the rest, she decides to put £20,000 in fixed-term bonds. She visits her library and gets help to check the rates online at MoneyFacts. One of the best for one year with monthly interest seems to be Birmingham Midshires paying 6.37%. Over three years, it is Lloyds TSB term deposit paying 6.25%. She goes into both branches next time she is in town. She decides to put half over one year and half over three years. Even though she is earning less over three years she is not sure where rates will be in a year's time so she likes to have some certainty over a bit longer. It also allows her to think about her money again in a year's time and see how she is managing and how much of her £4,000 is left in the Barclays saver account. Both bonds pay the income monthly and her income is well below her tax allowance, so she registers to have the income on those paid gross as well.

Commentary

Nooreen has thought about her money for the first time since Navtej died, and realises how much it has cost her to do nothing about it before. She has increased the income earned by her savings by over £1,100 a year and she now gets a regular £105.17 a month credited to her current account from her bonds. She can either take it out with a card or at the Post Office or make a phone call to move it straight to her savings account. The money in her savings account earns another £14.12 a month. She has stopped paying any tax. She has claimed Pension Credit, which boosts her pension by another £12.17 a week (more than £600 a year). She has never felt so well off since she was widowed. She can review her finances again next year when her first bond matures and again in three years. She has taken no risks except that the three year income may not look so good if interest rates rise a lot. She could also claim back some tax for previous years on form R40 from HM Revenue & Customs for the years when she should not have been paying tax on her savings. That cost her more than £35 a year. She gets form R40 for each year and receives a nice cheque from HMRC for around £200. She beats the banks – and the taxman!

5. Ed and Meg

Ed and Meg have been married for 32 years and are both 60 years old. They pay £228 a month on their mortgage but that ends in five years' time. It is an endowment mortgage; but if the endowment does not cover the whole loan, Ed will have a lump sum from his company pension that will. Ed earns £32,000 a year. Meg has spent most of her life looking after the family, all of whom have now left home. Her outside jobs have been poorly paid without pensions and since she married at 28 she has paid the reduced married woman's NI contribution. They moved their current account to the Co-operative Bank about 20 years ago – partly for political reasons when Ed was getting very cross about Margaret Thatcher – and partly because there is a branch nearby. They keep a

Ed and Meg's original savings package

	Invested	Interest rate	Amount received	After tax	Notes
Current account	£1,000	0.00%	£0.00	£0.00	Co-op bank
Savings account	£25,000	1.36%	£340.00	£272.00	Halifax Liquid Gold
Total	£26,000		£340.00	£272.00	

balance of around £1,000 and also have £25,000 in an old Halifax Liquid Gold savings account which they opened because they liked Arthur Daly.

Ed and Meg beat the banks

Meg paid full National Insurance contributions for more than 10 years when she was young. She contacts The Pension Service and finds that is enough to get a pension of £24.05 a week, which includes some graduated retirement benefit she paid for in work in the early 1970s. As her 60th birthday was eight months ago, she claims it at once and is pleased that it is backdated to then – a nice cheque for more than £800, which Meg uses to pay for a lovely holiday for them both – and a regular income of her own. When Ed reaches 65, she will get a higher pension on his contributions, which will be paid instead of her own pension. But at least she will have had it for nearly five years.

Ed, meanwhile, checks up on his company pension scheme. He finds that the rules have changed since he last looked; he can put some more in and his employer will match it. He gets full tax relief on his contributions, so he opts to put in another £50 a month, which costs him £39 because he gets full tax relief. His employer matches it, so for an outlay of £39 a month, he gets a total of £100 a month paid into his pension fund.

Ed now turns to their current account. When he moved it to the Co-operative Bank it took ages. But he discovers that he can switch it over to a Smile account, which is owned by the Co-operative Bank – he still likes their ethical policies. He is happy to go online with his finances. That earns him 3% and he and Meg usually have about £1,000 in there, so it seems worthwhile. They register on form R85 to have half the interest paid gross, as Meg is a non-taxpayer.

Next step is a mini-cash ISA, and again they stick with Smile. The rate is good for Smile customers and they do like the Co-op. Ed puts the maximum £3,000 in his name and at 5.5% gets £165 a year tax-free.

Now they want to invest the rest. They know that Meg is a non-taxpayer – she can have £5,225 a year before tax is due (£5,435 in 2008/09), and her income at the moment is far less than that. So they decide that the rest will be in her name.

Ed wants to make the money grow – they don't need income from it, but he does want more cash when he retires. He reckons £3,000 in a cash ISA is enough; the rest he wants to grow as much as possible. In discussion with Meg, they decide to split it – half on the stock market and half in a safe growth product. For complete safety they choose a National Savings Capital Bond Series 28, which guarantees 5.3% growth per year. They invest £11,000 and after five years they will get back £14,240. The interest is paid gross and the money is invested in Meg's name so that they do not have to pay any tax on it. Ed insists that the other £11,000 goes in the stock market. He is confident that historically, shares do better than other investments. And the tumbling prices of the start of the twenty-first century seem to be over, despite a few wobbles in 2007. He does not want to miss out again. He does a lot of research and finally decides to go for low charges and a tracker

fund that follows the FTSE All Share index. No-one
knows how well it will do. Ed estimates he will
make 5% a year, but hopes for more. Ed and Meg
put £4,000 in the tracker fund in Ed's name as a
mini-stocks and shares ISA and the other £7,000
as a maxi-ISA in the same tracker fund in Meg's
name so that there is no risk of tax being paid. It
does not really make much difference with this
investment, but they feel happier.

	Invested	Interest rate	Amount received	After tax	Notes
Current account	£1,000	3.00%	£30.00	£27.00	Smile
Cash ISA	£3,000	5.50%	£165.00	£165.00	Smile
Fixed interest	£11,000	5.30%	£583.00	£583.00	National Savings Capital Bond Series 28 – paid at the end of five year
Total on cash				**£775.00**	
Extra pension for Meg			£1,250.60	£1,250.60	
Total so far			£2,028.60	**£2,025.60**	
Tracker ISA	£11,000	5.00%*	£550.00	£550.00	*estimate only, not guaranteed
Total	£26,000		£2,578.60	**£2,575.60**	**Ed and Meg could be £2,303.60 better off this year; that's £44.30 a week**

Commentary

Meg has gained more than £1,200 a year by claiming her own pension – many married women do not realise they may be entitled to one before their husband retires.

They have saved tax by using Meg's tax allowances and made all their cash work harder; on cash savings alone they are more than £500 a year better off. Some of the money saved has been put into Ed's pension – costing him £39 a month but getting £100 a month in there. They have moved some money to a riskier investment, the FTSE All Share tracker and if Ed gets the 5% a year growth on his tracker fund, then they will do a lot better, making them £550 a year more on their investments. Those gains have been stored up for when Ed retires in five years time.

Then, as retirement looms, they will be free to look again at their safe, fixed-interest investment, and they will be able to see if Ed's stock market gamble has paid off. Banks definitely beaten!

6. Mary and Sean

Mary and Sean are both 65 years old and have just retired with company pensions of £11,450 and £6,850, respectively. They both get a full State Pension because Mary always paid full National Insurance contributions rather than the married woman's stamp, and both get a bit extra from SERPS. So their income is a shade under £28,000 a year. Their endowment has matured and as they paid off their mortgage some time ago, the proceeds are all theirs. They both took a lump sum from their pension. So after some necessary expenses on the house, they have £35,000 to find a home for. They've never felt so rich!

They are at the age when they want extra income for holidays and leisure rather than capital growth. Their current account is with Nationwide, where they earn 4.25% on their credit balance, as their joint pensions are still more than £1,000 a month. They normally have around £1,000 in the account. They temporarily deposit the £35,000 in a Nationwide CashBuilder account they have had for some years. It earns only 2.6% and Sean wonders why it pays less than the current account. But he leaves it there while they decide what to do.

Mary and Sean's original savings package

	Invested	Interest rate	Amount received	After tax	Notes
Current account	£1,000	4.25%	£42.50	£34.00	Nationwide FlexAccount
Savings account	£35,000	2.60%	£910.00	£728.00	Nationwide Cashbuilder card
Total	£36,000		£952.50	£762.00	

Mary and Sean beat the banks

They consider an annuity, but the rate for two people at 65 does not produce the income they want. And it is a once-and-for-all decision that they do not feel ready to make.

As they love using their computer, they go for an Intelligent Finance current account – or rather Ed does. It pays them just 2.96% which is not a great rate, but Ed likes the name and they don't leave much in their current account so he doesn't think it will make much difference. They tend to keep around £1,000 in their current account, so they open it up with £900. Next, as they are both taxpayers they each decide to open a mini-cash ISA with the maximum £3,000. They argue about which to go for. Sean leaps for the best-buy tables and goes for the obscure Tipton & Coseley Building Society which pays 6.4%. Mary points out that the rate only lasts for six months but Sean says he will switch it then. Mary used to walk past the Yorkshire Building Society every day and liked the look of it. So she chooses that and earns 6.05% on her money.

They have plenty of capital and want to spend some of it in a methodical way. So they buy a gilt. They choose 8% Treasury Stock 2013. They have to pay £115 for each £100 of stock, and they buy 130 units for £14,950 (plus £69 in fees). That means they get an income of almost 7% on their investment. The downside is that, when they redeem it in 2013, they will only be given back £13,000 for their £14,950 of stock. In other words, they will have spent £1,950 of it over that period. But they don't mind. The tables in the newspaper show that it is a real return over the period of 5.2% before tax, with which they are happy. The income is paid gross in March and September. Income tax has to be paid on it, of course, but not until 31 January when they fill in their self-assessment forms.

That leaves them £14,150. They decide the best thing to do with that is to put it in cash ISAs each year, especially as the cash allowance rises to £3,600 in 2008. Meanwhile, they put it away for a year in a fixed-interest bond from Anglo Irish Bank. It pays 6.7%, which is taxable. They can review it in a year, putting another £7,200 between them in cash ISAs and then thinking what to do with the balance.

	Invested	Interest rate	Amount received	After tax	Notes
Current account	£900	2.96%	£26.64	£21.31	Intelligent Finance
Cash ISA, Sean	£3,000	6.22%	£186.60	£186.60	Tipton & Coseley BS Premier ISA – takes account of rate dip after six months
Cash ISA, Mary	£3,000	6.05%	£181.50	£181.50	Yorkshire BS
Gilt Treas. 8% 2013	£14,950		£1,040.00	£832.00	Paid in two instalments March and September
Fixed rate bond, one year	£14,150	6.70%	£948.05	£758.44	Anglo Irish Bank
Total	£36,000		£2,382.79	£1,979.85	**Mary and Sean are £1,217.85 a year better off; that's £23.42 a week**

Commentary

Mary and Sean have used their pension lump sums to increase their spending money but stay flexible. They have maximised tax-free income, tied up some money for a period, swapping some capital for cash now through the gilt, and making their current account earn money as well. They are a bank-beating £1,217 a year better off, although some of that is the return of capital on their gilt. Sean does not move his ISA after six months. So the real return on his money over a year is 6.22%. He says he will wait until next April when they can look at putting £7,200 more between them into a cash ISA and perhaps a bit into something more risky. In five years, their gilt matures and they can look at it again and may decide they are then old enough to realise some of the value of their home through an equity release scheme, or they could consider buying an annuity.

Summary

These six people have well and truly beaten the banks. They have done it in four ways:

- moved their current account so even that money is earning something

- got rid of old savings accounts that pay rubbish rates and moved to new ones, if possible tying up the money to squeeze a bit more out of it

- made sure that no unnecessary tax is paid on what their savings earn

- made sensible, low-risk investments where appropriate.

In addition, two of them have claimed a pension or pension credit they did not know they were entitled to.

And none of them has used – or paid – a financial adviser. More on that next.

Getting financial advice

Consumer protection

The Financial Services Authority (FSA) now regulates almost all the investment and savings products on the market as well as the people who sell them to us and the banks and financial companies that back them. It covers unit trusts, pension schemes, endowment policies, insurance and mortgages, including most equity release products, as well as more obscure things such as futures and options.

However, some investment and savings products are outside the scope of the FSA. They include National Savings products as well as current accounts with banks and building societies. Also excluded are investments in physical things, such as property, stamps, precious stones, antiques, cars and wine. If you buy shares directly, including shares in an investment trust or a REIT, you are not protected by the FSA. But any adviser or broker you buy the shares through will be regulated, and their advice will come under the FSA's rules. Mortgage advice, equity release and most general insurance products are also now regulated by the FSA.

The existence of the regulator does not mean that we do not have to be careful. Firms will still fail and crooks will still try to part us from our money. All investment will continue to carry some risk. Some firms which make money out of financial products are very clever at placing their product in the gaps between regulation; and without regulation, there is usually no compensation if things go horribly wrong. Nevertheless, having an effective regulator helps us to be more confident that the people who sell us financial products are trained and registered and that the companies behind financial products are sound and trustworthy. In addition, advertisements for financial products should be truthful and information about financial products clear and straightforward.

The regulator cannot protect us against human weakness – greed can still drive both parties to a financial deal and there will always be fools and knaves in financial institutions as elsewhere. If someone is determined to defraud investors, they will often succeed.

The Banking Code

Just about all banks and building societies subscribe to the Banking Code which sets down the basic principles of fair dealing which they have to follow. The Code is run by a Standards Board with representatives of the banks and building societies, consumer groups and academics. It used to be revised every two years but in a retrograde step, this was recently lengthened to once every three years. The banks are very good at misleading customers and making money out of them without actually breaking the Code but it is better than nothing. For example, it forced the banks to tell customers when they cut an interest rate on a savings account. And it introduced clearer information about the charges on credit cards.

You can complain to the Board if you think the Code has not been followed and it does no harm to let it know when you have been treated unfairly.

Choosing an adviser

The regulation and organisation of financial advice changed from 1 June 2005, changed again in November 2007 and will change yet again in 2009. It is still not clear what the end result will be.

At the moment, financial advisers can work in three different ways:

- **Tied** – they work for one company such as a bank or insurance company and only sell its products

- **Multi-tied** – they look at products from a panel of providers, maybe half a dozen, and can only sell the products of the companies on that panel. From time to time, the companies on their panel may change

- **Whole of market** – they look at products from the whole market – or at least a large representative sample – and find the one that suits you best.

Never use a financial adviser who is not 'whole of market'. If you discover that an adviser is tied or multi-tied do not even consider following their recommendations. They cannot give you the best advice because they are confined to the products of one or a few banks, insurance companies and investment funds.

Until November 2007, advisers had to give you a document at the start of your discussions called Key Facts about our Services. That explained which of these three sorts of adviser they were, under the heading, 'Whose products do we offer?' This document is no longer compulsory and not all advisers will give you one but they still have to make it clear whether they are whole of market, offer the products of a few companies, or offer products from just one company.

Even among whole of market advisers there is another division. To call themselves 'independent' they have to let you pay by a fee rather than earning their money from commission. A few only charge fees but all advisers who call themselves independent must at least offer that option.

So your first question is 'Are you an independent financial adviser'. **If the answer is anything but 'Yes', walk away.**

Just to confuse you further, independent financial advisers are divided into three other groups:

- those that give advice and recommendations

- those who are junior and possibly unqualified and who only advise on a limited range of 'stakeholder' products

- those that just do what you ask them to do, with no advice.

If you want advice, then only ever consider those who give advice and recommendations. The junior bunch, who are rare among independents, may be cheaper but they can only advise you on a narrow range of specific products such as ISAs or stakeholder pensions that may or may not be right for you. Ask for someone else.

The third group, who offer no advice – despite calling themselves advisers – are only there because many insurance and investment companies – called 'product providers' in the jargon – will only sell some products through intermediaries. So these (non)advisers sit there buying what you tell them and passing it on to you. They call this 'execution only' business. Only use them if you really know what you want.

You may be given a *Key Facts* document setting all this out or you may not. But they should still make it clear how they work. If you are in any doubt ask the question: 'Do you give advice?'

If you want financial advice, you should always use an independent financial adviser (IFA) who is qualified and who gives advice. Sometimes they call themselves 'financial planners'. That term has no legal meaning. So always ask if they are 'independent', which means that they are obliged by law to find you the best deal for your circumstances. Even among independents, some will be better than others. But financial advisers who are not independent are not worth considering, because they are limited by law in what they can tell you and sell you.

Future changes

The Financial Services Authority is consulting on major changes to the way investment products are sold. Under these plans, the word 'independent' may be extended to advisers who are tied or multi-tied if they meet certain other criteria. The FSA may also divide financial advice into expensive, professional financial planning for people who can afford it, general advice for those with less to spend, and what it is calling 'Primary Advice' for those with limited resources. The FSA's final ideas will become known in 2008 and no change is expected until 2009 at the earliest.

Commission

Most IFAs still earn most of their money by taking commission on the final sale. So if they sell you nothing, they earn nothing. How much they earn depends in part on what they sell you – some products are far more profitable than others. Under the law, the commission they might earn plays no part in the advice IFAs give. But human nature being what it is, the customers certainly feel it does, and research done by the Financial Services Authority and the Association of British Insurers shows that in some cases it in fact does.

At the time of writing, all IFAs have to offer you the choice of paying a fee instead. That is always the best option. Even if you have to borrow the money over a year or two, it is better to pay the fee upfront. You should not be fooled by offers to let it be paid by 'offsetting' it against commission. That just means it is a fee you are paying over many years which can have a devastating effect on your investment. If you pay a fee, the commission should be paid back to you, usually by boosting your investment.

Most IFAs who charge fees will give you one free session to see if both sides think it is worth pursuing matters. If an adviser won't do that, go elsewhere. Once you get into paid time, £100 an hour is at the lower end of the scale. You will pay more in cities and wealthier parts of the UK. The fee will have to be paid whether you buy a product or not. But if you do buy something, the fee will almost certainly be less than the commission you would have paid.

If you really cannot afford a fee, you should ask yourself if you need financial advice of this sort at all.

Finding advice

It is illegal for anyone to sell or offer advice about investments, mortgages, or most insurance without being registered to do so or working for a company that is registered. If you buy products from an unregistered person or company, then you are not covered by the protection and compensation schemes that exist. You can check with the FSA if a company or a qualified adviser is registered – see page 105.

Despite their name, financial advisers will not usually be able to advise you on debt, borrowing, credit cards, benefits or bank accounts. People who do advise on those things generally do not have to be registered or qualified.

You can get a list of IFAs in your local area from the Internet on www.unbiased.co.uk. That website allows you to specify the kind of adviser you want and the qualifications he or she (and you can say which you would prefer) has.

Alternatively, you might get a recommendation from a friend who has similar financial needs to yours and has a trusted adviser who has done well for them over a period of time.

You should always insist that your first visit to an IFA is at their office. You are more in control than if they come to your home – it is very hard to ask someone to leave if they are on your sofa drinking tea. Try out two or three – remember that the first interview will be free – to see if you like them and understand what they say. Once you have established that they are independent and can advise and make recommendations, it is time to ask the difficult questions, such as:

- Do you specialise in any particular areas, such as pensions or advice for people over 50? (Make sure they say 'Yes' to whatever particular things you are interested in.)

- What experience and qualifications do you have for that specialisation? (If they do not have experience and extra qualifications in this topic, then leave.)

- How many clients do you personally deal with? (If the answer is a very large number, can you be sure that you will get the attention you should?)

- Can I speak to a couple of them? (If the adviser will not put you in touch with other customers, walk away.)

If you do not like the answers you get or the attitude of the adviser, leave. Finance is a very personal business and it is essential that you like and trust the people you deal with.

Brace yourself

Visiting a financial adviser is always an unfair battle. The adviser will have been doing it for years and know the answers to all the obvious questions. The adviser is the professional, you are the amateur. So the more you prepare and practise the more likely you are to come out with a good result.

The adviser's first job should be to find out about you. What do you need from your money? They will also talk to you about risk. Often by asking your 'attitude' to it or what is your 'risk profile'? The big mistake many advisers make at this point is to imply that 'risk means reward' or talk about the 'risk reward trade off'. They imply that if you have a bit of courage and take a riskier investment you will make more money than if you are cautious. Rubbish! Of course you might – but risk means risk. If you take a risk you could lose some or even all of your money. And you certainly could make a very poor return. Otherwise, there would be no risk.

Instead of answering questions – especially ones you do not know the answer to – why not ask them? After all, the IFA is the adviser not you!

Ask:

• Why is this investment or plan right for me?

- What will I get out of the deal? At best? At worst?

- What will you get out of the deal?

- Could I lose money?

- What are the alternatives?

- How does this investment compare with the products of National Savings?

- Why is this better than putting my money in a savings account earning 6%?

Always be on your guard. Most financial advisers earn their money through commission. That creates a conflict of interest between them and you – their interest may be to sell you the most profitable product.

So:

- Be suspicious of any promise of exceptional returns: if a deal sounds too good to be true, it probably is.

- Never be bamboozled into investing in a scheme you don't understand – particularly if the adviser is vague about the details or does not seem to understand it themselves.

- Don't be panicked into parting with your money because the adviser says that you must take advantage of a special offer immediately.

- Beware if you are told to cash in all your investments so that the adviser can invest them elsewhere – he or she may be recycling investments unnecessarily in order to boost commission. This process, known as 'churning', is not legal but is not uncommon either.

- Be very suspicious of an adviser who tells you to put all your money into one investment. That breaks the key rule, which is to spread your investments.

- Make your cheque out to the firm your money will be invested in, not the financial adviser. If you are asked to do so, walk away, no matter what reason is given.

- Keep up-to-date by reading the financial sections of newspapers and magazines, listening to radio programmes such as Money Box on Radio 4 and watching television programmes such as Working Lunch on BBC 2.

All advisers should tell you how much fee or commission they will get. If they are reluctant, then walk away. Until recently, all advisers had to give you a standard document comparing the commission they charge on certain products to the market average and what that might mean in terms of earnings from selling you those standard products. These rules have now gone. But good advisers will give it you anyway.

Advisers are still required to tell you clearly about the product's 'key features' – its aims, risks and benefits, as well as the impact of charges and expenses. A personal illustration must also be given, showing projected costs and fund growth based on the customer's personal circumstances.

The adviser must also provide you with a 'reason why' letter, explaining why the product is right for you. Read this letter carefully and make sure that it summarises accurately the conversation you had with them. In particular that it reflects your views of how much risk you are prepared to take with your money. Although risk does not always mean reward for you, it normally does for the adviser. The more risk you take, the more commission the adviser will be paid.

You normally have a period in which you can cancel the deal without penalty. You must be told clearly what this cooling-off period is. Don't be afraid to cancel the deal in that time if you are not completely happy with it. Don't feel obliged to buy something from the person because they seemed nice or needed the sale.

Insurance

When you buy a financial product of any sort – an investment, a credit card, a loan, a bank account, a pension – the chances are the financial adviser will try to sell you insurance as well. There is one simple reason for that – to make more money.

Of course, insurance may be a good idea. But always ask yourself what is the financial risk I am insuring myself against? If that risk happens, what will the policy actually pay me, bearing in mind my age, employment status and health? Is the price I am being asked to pay reasonable for that cover?

Life insurance – which you may quite sensibly have paid for when you were younger – is often not needed at all once you get older and have no financial dependants. Other profitable lines that advisers will try to flog you include critical illness cover – usually completely inappropriate as you get older (and generally a waste of money even when you are younger) and a whole panoply of items to insure you for everything from ID theft to payment protection. Generally, they are all best avoided – especially when you reach pension age.

Complaining

If you believe that you have been sold an inappropriate investment, or that a financial firm has been negligent, incompetent or downright dishonest, there is a set procedure for dealing with complaints, which all registered financial firms have to follow.

First, you should write to the Chief Executive of the company setting out clearly your complaint and what you want done about it. If your complaint is not dealt with to your satisfaction within eight weeks, your case has reached what is called 'deadlock' and you can go to the Financial Ombudsman Service.

Ombudsman

You can complain to the Financial Ombudsman Service (FOS) about any financial firm, such as a bank or investment company, that is registered with the FSA. For example, you may have been sold the wrong product for your age or needs, or sold one without the risks being explained. Or you may just feel that your bank has mishandled your instructions over a direct debit or standing order. You have six months from the time your case is 'deadlocked' to go to the FOS.

In many cases, the Ombudsman Service will resolve the problem quickly by finding a compromise acceptable to both sides. If that is not possible, the case proceeds to a formal investigation and a decision. Normally, the company will accept that. If either you or the company does not accept the decision, either of you can appeal to an Ombudsman. Once the Ombudsman gives a formal ruling, which can include compensation to the customer, the company has to follow it. There is no appeal to the courts, although some companies have tried unsuccessfully to find ways to get the courts to overturn the Ombudsman's decision.

The Financial Ombudsman Service is free for you, though the company you complain about will normally have to pay a fee of a few hundred pounds. Most people can manage the complaint themselves. You do not need a lawyer to argue your case, and beware of claims-handling companies who offer to take you through the process of complaining in return for a hefty slice – plus VAT – of any compensation you get.

The FOS is not a consumer rights service. It is there to resolve disputes and in many cases the outcome will be a compromise. If you disagree with the ruling or the compensation ordered, you can still go to court, although that is likely to be stressful, expensive and time-consuming.

Compensation

The FOS can order a company to pay compensation. But if the company has gone out of business, the Financial Services Compensation Scheme (FSCS) steps in and pays the compensation. It can also step in if a firm goes out of business taking clients' money with it.

The maximum amount of compensation the FSCS pays varies vary from one sort of financial product to another:

- If you lose money from a bank or building society account, you now get 100% of the first £35,000. Anything above that is not covered.

- Cash savings which were in Northern Rock on 19 September 2007 were covered at 100% up to any amount after the crisis the bank experienced that month. In October 2007, this guarantee was extended to savings put into the bank in the future as well. At some point, this limitless guarantee will be withdrawn by the Government.

- If an insurance claim is not met because an insurer has gone bust, you get 100% of the first £2,000 and 90% of the rest.

- If an investment company goes bust, the maximum compensation is £48,000.

You normally have to ask for compensation within six years of the company going out of business.

This scheme applies only to firms regulated by the FSA. Some investment firms in the UK do not have to be regulated and are not covered by the scheme. If you invest in a company based in another country, even if the product was sold to you in the UK, you may have to rely on the compensation scheme in that country. And if you are foolish enough to do business in the UK with a firm which should be regulated but is not, then no compensation will be due.

More help

Benefits, Pensions and Tax

Government information
www.direct.gov.uk
This website is becoming the one-stop-shop for all information on Government services in the UK, including details on benefits, social security and tax.

The Pension Service
Whitley Road
Newcastle upon Tyne
NE98 1BA
0845 600 2537
www.thepensionservice.gov.uk
Information service for tracing pensions: tracing pensions, pension credits, winter fuel payments and lots more.

The Pensions Advisory Service (TPAS)
11 Belgrave Road
London SW1V 1RB
Helpline: 0845 601 2923
www.pensionadvisory service.org.uk
For questions and complaints about pensions.

Unclaimed Assets Register
www.uar.co.uk
Holds information about insurance policies and financial products that have not been claimed. Charges a fee.

Entitled to?
www.entitledto.co.uk
An amazing website that works out entitlement to means-tested benefits including Pension Credit, tax credits, Council Tax Benefit and Housing Benefit.

Redundancy payments office
Customer Service Unit
7th Floor, 83–85 Hagley House
Birmingham B16 8QG
Helpline: 0845 145 00 04
www.reducdancyhelp.co.uk
For information about matters relating to redundancy.

The Pension Service
0845 60 60 265
www.thepensionservice.gov.uk
The part of the Department for Work and Pensions that deals with state pensions.

Banking

British Bankers Association
Dormant Account Unit
020 7216 8909
www.bba.org.uk
The trade body of banks in the UK. Can help you trace money in forgotten bank accounts.

Building Societies Association
3 Savile Row
London W1S 3PB
020 7437 0655
www.bsa.org.uk
The trade association for all building societies.

Link
www.link.co.uk
Find out your nearest free cash machine.

APACS The UK payments association
www.apacs.org.uk
Responsible for the computers that move money around the banking system. Advice on security and ID theft. At some point there will be information about the new instant clearing for telephone and Internet banking when it starts in 2008.

Debt

Consumer Credit Counselling Service

Wade House
Merrion Centre
Leeds LS2 8NG
0800 138 1111
www.cccs.co.uk
Free impartial advice for anyone with a debt problem.

The Insolvency Service

Insolvency: 020 7291 6895
Redundancy: 0845 145 0004
www.insolvency.gov.uk
Government department that deals with bankruptcy and insolvency.

National Debtline

0808 808 4000
www.nationaldebtline.co.uk
Offers free debt advice and produces factsheets, which are free to individuals in debt.

Financial advice

Advice Guide

www.adviceguide.org.uk
A general advice website run by Citizens Advice.

Money Made Clear

www.moneymadeclear.fsa.gov.uk
A good and improving website from the Financial Services Authority. Useful guides and information, details of scams, current news. Overall trustworthy if a little dull at times.

FSA comparative tables

www.fsa.gov.uk/tables
The regulator's comparison site for some financial products. For information only – no through purchases possible.

Adviser check

0845 606 1234
www.fsa.gov.uk/register/indivSearchForm.do
Check if a financial adviser or firm is registered with the FSA.

Unbiased.co.uk

Hotline: 0800 085 3250
www.unbiased.co.uk
Phone their hotline for a list of independent financial advisers in your home or work area.

Moneysavingexpert

www.moneysavingexpert.
com

A quirky website offering practical advice on saving money. It has useful sections on best-buys for financial products, up-to-date advice on getting your own back on the financial services industry and chatrooms.

The Motley Fool

www.fool.co.uk

Another useful website for financial advice and information with its own best-buy tables.

MoneyFacts

www.moneyfacts.com

The first and probably still the best of the comparison sites for bank accounts, credit cards, loans and mortgages. Also published as a monthly magazine.

Moneysupermarket.
com

www.moneysupermarket.
com

A commercial website for comparing and buying financial products and services.

Find

www.find.co.uk

Information on a lot of financial products as well as lists of online discount brokers.

Insurance

Association of British Insurers

020 7600 3333

www.abi.org.uk

Offers advice and information on a wide range of insurance products. Runs a quality-mark scheme called Raising Standards, which assesses financial services products – see their website: www.raisingstandards.net for more information.

British Insurance Brokers' Association (BIBA)

14 Bevis Marks
London EC3A 7NT
Helpline: 0870 950 1790
www.biba.org.uk

The leading UK trade association for general insurance brokers.

Investing

Debt Management Office (DMO)
020 7862 6500
www.dmo.gov.uk
Administers gilts for the Government and produces free guides for private investors.

The Ethical Investment Association
www.ethicalinvestment.
  org.uk
Can put you in touch with financial advisers who are committed to finding you ethical investments.

Ethical Investment Research Service
020 7840 5700
www.eiris.org
Publishes a range of publications, including a guide to choosing a financial adviser.

UK Social Investment Forum
020 7405 0040
www.uksif.org
For information on socially responsible investment.

ProShare Clubs
www.proshareclubs.co.uk
The source for joining or forming a share investment club. Beware its phone line which charges 60p a minute.

Regulators

Financial Ombudsman Service (FOS)
Helpline: 0845 080 1800
*www.financial-
  ombudsman.org.uk*
Provides consumers with a free independent service for resolving disputes with financial firms.

The Financial Services Authority (FSA)
020 7066 1000
Helpline: 0845 606 1234
www.fsa.gov.uk
Regulates most investments and financial service providers.

Financial Services Compensation Scheme (FSCS)
020 7892 7300
www.fscs.org.uk
Pays compensation to customers of financial services companies that go out of business.

Consumer Direct
08454 040506
www.consumerdirect.
    gov.uk
Funded by the Office of Fair Trading and works in partnership with Local Authority Trading Standards Services.

Trading Standards Central
www.tradingstandards.
    gov.uk
A lot of information about consumer rights and how to complain as well as links to local trading standards offices.

The Banking Code Standards Board
0845 230 9694
www.bankingcode.org.uk
Produces and enforces the Code of Practice that just about all banks and building societies in the UK must follow.

Saving

National Savings & Investments
0845 964 5000
www.nsandi.com
The Investors' Guide and other National Savings & Investments leaflets can be found here or at some Post Offices. Contact for help with finding lost NS&I savings accounts.

Tax

Her Majesty's Revenue & Customs
www.hmrc.gov.uk
Everything you need to know about tax in the UK, though not always as clear or easy to find your way around as it might be. Look under 'Her Majesty's …' in the business section of your local phone book. If it is not there, try under 'Inland Revenue', which is where it used to be.
Also:
Taxback: 0845 077 6543
Pay less tax on your savings: 0845 980 0645.

Low Incomes Tax Reform Group

020 7235 9381
Helpline: 0845 601 3321
www.litrg.org.uk
Lobbies for simplification of the tax system and speaks for those unfairly treated by the tax system.

TaxAid

020 7803 4959
(10am–noon, Mon–Thurs)
www.taxaid.org.uk
Offers free advice, on the telephone or by appointment only, to people with tax problems who cannot afford an accountant.

Tax Help for Older People

0845 601 3321.
www.taxvol.org.uk
An independent tax advice service for older people on low incomes who cannot afford to pay for professional help.

Publications and broadcasts

Magazines and newspapers

Personal finance sections are in daily newspapers on Wednesday or Saturday and most Sunday newspapers carry them too.

Financial Times *carries Stock Exchange and other market prices and money market funds.*
www.ft.com

Investors Chronicle *has simply-written articles on companies in the news, and topical articles of interest to investors.*
www.investorschronicle
.co.uk

MoneyFacts *is a monthly publication giving interest rates for all financial products.*
0870 2250 100
www.moneyfacts.co.uk

Moneywise *is a monthly magazine giving financial information in an easy-to-read, lively format. Available from newsagents.*
www.moneywise.co.uk

Saga Magazine *has six pages each month on finance, investment and money.*
www.saga.co.uk/money

Money Management *contains hugely detailed tables showing performance statistics for pensions and other investments.*
www.ftadviser.com

Radio and television programmes

Money Box – *a weekly personal finance news programme on BBC Radio 4 on Saturday at noon, repeated Sunday at 9pm. Listen on the web at any time or download a podcast at:*
www.bbc.co.uk/
    moneybox

Money Box Live – *a weekly personal finance phone-in answering questions on various topics throughout the year. BBC Radio 4 on Monday at 3pm. Listen on the web at anytime or download a podcast at:*
www.bbc.co.uk/
    moneybox

Working Lunch – *a personal finance and investment programme. BBC Two, weekday lunchtimes.*
www.bbc.co.uk/
    workinglunch

Index

About Age Concern

Age Concern is the UK's largest organisation working for and with older people to enable them to make more of life. We are a federation of over 400 independent charities who share the same name, values and standards and believe that later life should be fulfilling, enjoyable and productive.

Age Concern England
1268 London Road
London SW16 4ER
SW16 4ER
Tel: 020 8765 7200
www.ageconcern.org.uk

Age Concern Cymru
Ty John Pathy
Units 13 and 14 Neptune Court
Vanguard Way, Cardiff CF24 5PJ
Tel: 029 2043 1555
www.accymru.org.uk

Age Concern Scotland
Causewayside House
160 Causewayside
Edinburgh EH9 1PP
Tel: 0845 833 0200
www.ageconcernscotland.org.uk

Age Concern Northern Ireland
3 Lower Crescent
Belfast BT7 1NR
Tel: 028 9024 5729
www.ageconcernni.org

Age Concern Books

Age Concern publishes a wide range of bestselling books that help thousands of people each year. They provide practical, trusted advice on subjects ranging from pensions and planning for retirement, to using a computer and surfing the internet. Whether you are caring for someone with a health problem or want to know more about your rights to healthcare, we have something for everyone.

Ordering is easy To order any of our books or request our free catalogue simply choose one of the following options:

☎ **Call us on 0870 44 22 120**

 **Visit our website at www.ageconcern.org.uk/bookshop**

 **Email us at sales@ageconcernbooks.co.uk**

You can also buy our books from all good bookshops.

Another great book from Age Concern...

How to be a Silver Surfer, 3rd Edition
A beginner's guide to the internet
Emma Aldridge

This bestselling guide is perfect for people who are new to the internet and apprehensive about how to use it. User-friendly with full colour illustrations and simple step-by-step explanations throughout, this book makes getting online so easy, readers will be surfing the net in no time.

£7.99 • Paperback • 978-0-86242-421-3

Ordering is easy

To order any of our books or request our free catalogue simply choose one of the following options:

☎ **Call us on 0870 44 22 120**

🖱 **Visit our website at www.ageconcern.org.uk/bookshop**

✉ **Email us at sales@ageconcernbooks.co.uk**

You can also buy our books from all good bookshops.